Medicinal Herbs And Poisonous Plants /by David Ellis

PREFACE

In the course of his work the writer comes in contact with a large number of people who are interested in Botany as a recreation and a change from the work by which they make their living. It is noteworthy with such students that interest in a plant is considerably quickened when it can be shown that the plant in question possesses either medicinal or poisonous properties. This would seem to indicate the need for a book which would impart useful information and at the same time emphasize the paramount importance of scientific training. Since the outbreak of the present War the number of amateur botanists in large centres like Glasgow has considerably increased. The interest of some has been aroused by the patriotic efforts of such organizations as the National Herb-growing Association; others, having become plot-holders, deem a scientific groundwork in Botany a matter of urgent necessity; still others are attracted by the enhanced prices paid for drugs which before the War were imported from Germany because we could not be bothered, or because it did not pay, to cultivate or collect the plants in this country. Hence, in the case of the more important British drug plants, after the salient features have been described, an account is given of the cultivation, source of supply, present and former price, and other details bearing upon the commercial aspect of the subject. In this connection the author has received much help from Mr. Wren, of Messrs. Potter & Clarke, who has kindly allowed his knowledge to be laid under contribution. Among medicinal plants have been included the various herbs that are imported or collected for the herbalist. Whilst the medicinal value of a large number of these herbs must be regarded as very doubtful, the fact that many of them are imported by the ton suggests that, to many people at any rate, they rank as medicinal plants, although their insertion in these pages is a concession to their commercial rather than their intrinsic value.

A work descriptive of poisonous plants obviously calls for no apology. It is justified from the point of view of personal protection alone. When one realizes the awful things which children attempt to masticate and swallow, the dissemination of a knowledge of poisonous plants seems a necessity. Again, even in these days, dabbling in herbs for curative purposes is by no means uncommon, and to the eyes of those ignorant of Botany several quite different plants appear to be identical. This occasionally gives rise to serious mistakes.

The diagrams have been drawn with a view to enabling the student to identify the plant in the field by fixing attention on the most outstanding features in its structure, or on some marked peculiarity exhibited by the plant. Such helps are invaluable in field work, and greatly facilitate the subsequent process of finding the Natural Order to which any particular plant belongs.

An inclusion of all the plants that at one time or another have been regarded as possessing medicinal properties would embrace a very large number of plants that are now known to be worthless, and so these are not mentioned. The scope of the present work also does not allow of the treatment of the medicinal or poisonous plants that are found among the Cryptogams.

It was deemed expedient to place under a separate chapter all those poisonous and medicinal plants which grow as trees or large shrubs, even though this necessitated grouping together a collection of plants drawn from the four corners of the phanerogamic kingdom. This plan was found to be the more convenient because it made possible the introduction into the text of the Gymnosperms that possessed medicinal properties. In themselves their small number did not justify the inclusion of the Gymnosperms in the Tables of Classification, more especially as their inclusion would have added considerably to the complexity of the Tables.

In the preparation of this book the chief writers whose publications were laid under contribution were Holmes, Shenstone, Sowerby, Greenish, Southall, Bentham and Hooker, Glaister, and Henslow. Finally, my grateful thanks are due to Miss Margaret Irwin for revising my manuscript, and to my wife for help in preparing the diagrams.

DAVID ELLIS.

Royal Technical College,
Glasgow.

CONTENTS

CHAPTER I

CHAPTER II

CHAPTER III

MONOCOTYLEDONS

CHAPTER IV

DICOTYLEDONS: INCOMPLETÆ

CHAPTER V

DICOTYLEDONS: POLYPETALÆ I

CHAPTER VI

DICOTYLEDONS: POLYPETALÆ II

CHAPTER VII

DICOTYLEDONS: GAMOPETALÆ I

CHAPTER VIII

DICOTYLEDONS: GAMOPETALÆ II

CHAPTER IX

DICOTYLEDONS: GAMOPETALÆ III

CHAPTER X

TREES AND SHRUBS

MEDICINAL HERBS AND POISONOUS PLANTS

CHAPTER I

THE STRUCTURE OF THE FLOWER

Some knowledge of the structure of flowers is a necessary qualification for the study of poisonous and medicinal plants, for many plants can be identified by their flowers, and in many cases difficulties of identification can be solved by an appeal to the flower. Let us take for an example a common flower like the Buttercup and dissect it. The reader should compare a living specimen of this flower with fig. 1 and make certain that he can identify all the parts.

Each complete *flower* consists of four different structures arranged in whorls at the apex of a stalk. The two outermost beginning from the outside are called respectively the *calyx* and the *corolla*. The calyx consists of *sepals*, and the corolla of *petals*. Thus in the Buttercup the calyx consists of five green sepals, and the corolla of five yellow petals. Inside the corolla are the *stamens*; each of these is composed of a stalk which supports at its end an expanded structure called the *anther*. The last-named contains the *pollen grains*; these are liberated when ripe by the splitting of the anther. In the Buttercup the stamens are numerous.

Removing the stamens, a small globular head will be left behind. This is the *pistil,* which in this case is not a single body, but is made up of an aggregation of similar structures. Each of these is called a *carpel.* We therefore speak of the pistil of the Buttercup being composed of numerous carpels.

The characters of the Buttercup may therefore be tabulated as follows:—

1. **Calyx.** Five green *sepals.*
2. **Corolla.** Five yellow *petals.*
3. Numerous **stamens.**
4. **Pistil.** Numerous *carpels.*

It will be further observed that the different parts of the flower are not in any way united either with themselves or with any other parts of the flower, e.g. each petal is free not only from the other petals but also from the sepals and stamens on either side of it.

We may take the Foxglove for our next example. The structure of this flower is quite different, there being considerable union among its component parts.

Examining as we did the Buttercup, we find the flower to be made up as follows:—

1. **Calyx.** Five united green *sepals.*
2. **Corolla.** Five united purplish *petals.*
3. **Stamens** Four in number, attached to the petals.
4. **Pistil.** Two completely united *carpels.*

It becomes necessary at this point to explain in greater detail the difference between the *pistil* and the *carpel.* This can best be done by comparing the pistils of the two flowers which we have already described. In the case of the Buttercup (see figs. 1 and 2) each one of the little structures (fig. 2) which compose the central part of the flower is called a *carpel.* There are about

20 or 30 of them in each Buttercup (fig. 1). Collectively they form the *pistil*. Hence we say that the pistil of the Buttercup is composed of 20 or 30 carpels, just as we

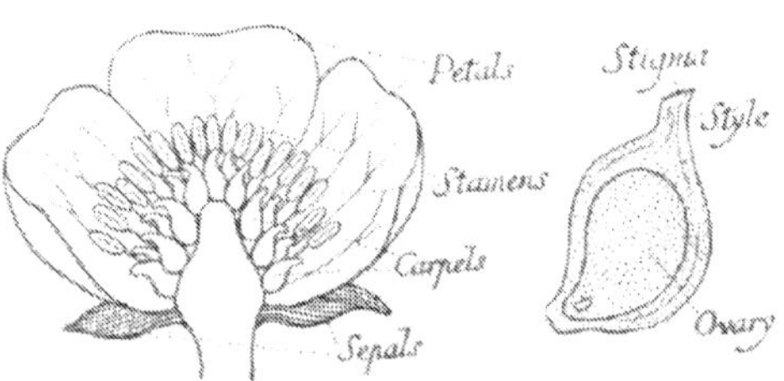

Fig. 1.—Section of Flower of Buttercup

Fig. 2.—Enlarged Section of Carpel

say that a *class* is composed of 20 or 30 *students*. Each carpel is made up of three parts:—

1. *Stigma*, or the top part, usually rough or sticky: in consequence it receives and detains the pollen grains. It often takes the shape of a small knob as in the Primrose, but this is not the case in the Buttercup.
2. *Style*, or the neck upon which the stigma is carried.
3. *Ovary*, or the lower expanded portion. This contains a cavity in which, in this case, a single *ovule* is developed. The ovule later develops into the *seed* (fig. 2).

The distinction between the terms *carpel* and *pistil* is not so easy to perceive in the case of the Foxglove flower. Here the number of carpels forming the pistil is only two, but these two are joined together (fig. 4). The evidence for the statement that the pistil is made up of two carpels is furnished by an examination of the top of the pistil, for there are seen to be two stigmas (fig. 4). Again, if the ovary be cut open, two cavities are observed. Strictly speaking, the ovary of the Foxglove is made up of two ovaries joined together; it is, in fact, a *compound ovary*. In the same way the style is really

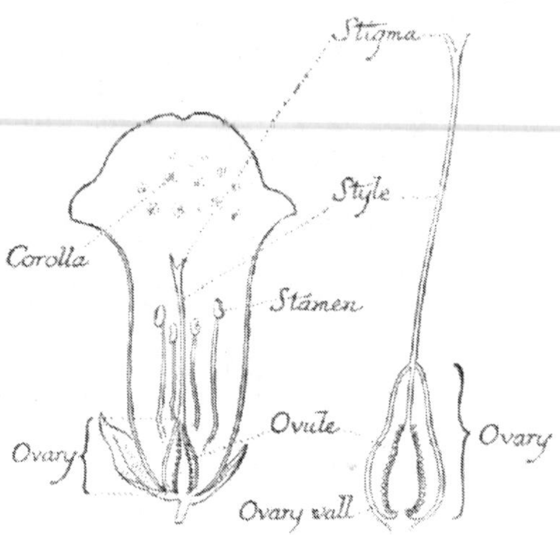

Fig. 3.—Section of Foxglove Flower

Fig. 4.—Enlarged Section of Pistil

compound, being made up of two styles joined together. In describing the pistil of the Foxglove, we should say that it is composed of two carpels. The ovaries and

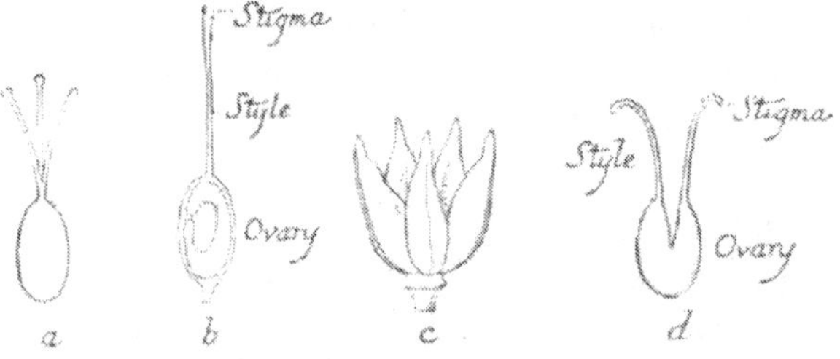

Fig. 5.—Various Types of Pistils

styles of these two carpels are completely united in this pistil, but the two stigmas (or stigmata) are free. In other plants it will be found that the number of carpels composing the pistil is not the same, and that the degree of union of the carpels is different. In fig. 5 a few types of pistils are given, and they should be carefully studied, for the classification of the higher plants depends largely on differences in the number and mode of union of the carpels.

The Snowdrop will supply us with our third example. Examining as before, we find it to be constructed as follows:—

1. **Calyx.** Three white *sepals.*
2. **Corolla.** Three white *petals.*
3. Six **stamens.**
4. **Pistil.** Three *carpels.*

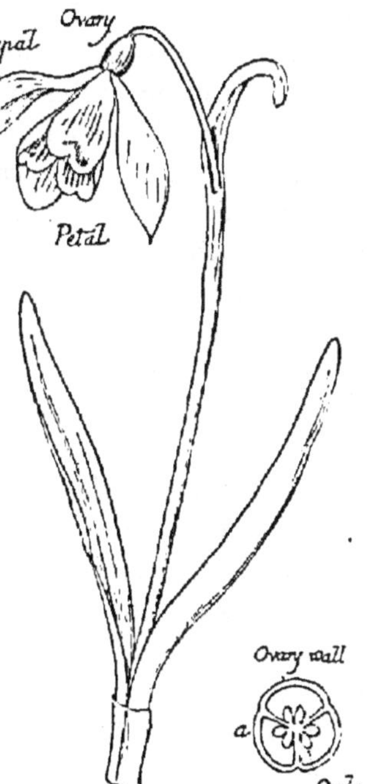

Fig. 6.—The Snowdrop
a, Section of ovary.

As is shown in fig. 6, the ovary in this flower is situated below the other parts of the flower. In this case the ovary is said to be *inferior*; in the flowers examined above, the ovary is said to be *superior*: it is enveloped by, not situated underneath, the calyx and corolla.

The reasons for the statement that the pistil is composed of three carpels should be carefully examined by the student. The first reason is furnished by the ovary, which, if cut open, shows three cavities (fig. 6, *a*); the second by the stigma, which is made up of three lobes closely joined together.

There is still another feature of interest in this flower, namely the prominence of the calyx. It is popularly supposed that the most conspicuous outer parts of a flower must necessarily be the corolla. As a matter of fact, whilst this is the case in the majority of flowers, it is not safe to rely on it; the safest rule to follow is to ascribe to the calyx the outer members, and to the corolla the inner members irrespective of their appearance. In the Snowdrop, for instance, an examination will show that three of the so-called petals are placed outside of the other three; the inner three must therefore be regarded as petals, and the outer three as sepals.

Finally, we must mention the differences in the flowers brought about by differences in the shape of the *receptacle*. This is the name given to that part of the flower-stalk which bears the floral parts. In most flowers the receptacle is just the rounded convex end of the stalk (fig. 7, *a*). On such a structure the pistil rises from the summit, the other floral parts arising successively immediately below it. A flower of this kind is said to be *hypogynous*. In other flowers the receptacle takes the form of a *cup* (fig. 7, *c*) or a *saucer* (fig. 7, *b*). In both forms the pistil arises from the centre of the cup or saucer, whilst the other floral parts spring from the rims. These flowers are said to be *perigynous*. In another type of perigyny, the stamens, corolla, and calyx are attached to a disk which encircles the ovary. This is shown diagrammatically in fig. 7, *d*. The disk may be at the top, or middle, or basal part of the ovary.

The *epigynous* flowers form a third type. These are flowers in which the receptacle has been hollowed out as shown in fig. 7, *e*, but an advance has been made in that the receptacle has fused with the ovary, so much so that it has become impossible to separate the wall of the ovary

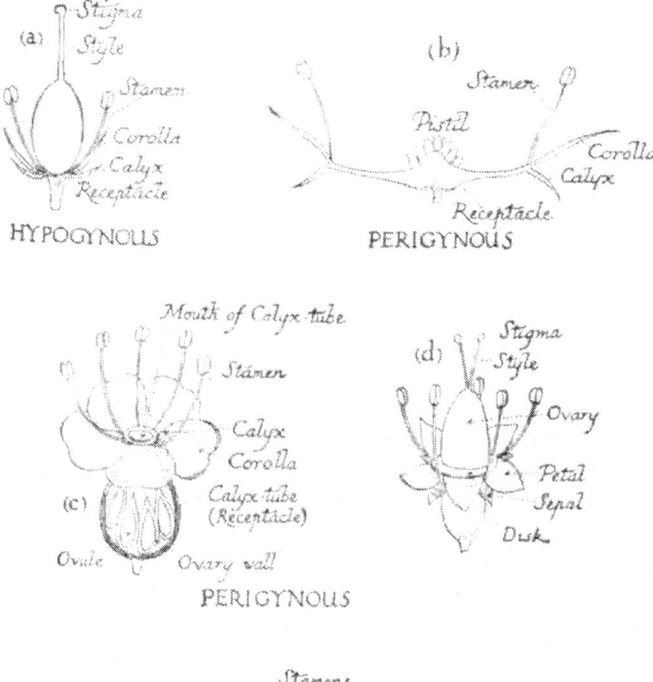

Fig. 7.—Various Types of Receptacles

from the receptacle, and hence it appears as though the stamens, petals, and sepals are inserted upon the ovary. A diagrammatic representation is shown in fig. 7, *e*. All the flowers with an inferior ovary belong to this type.

A good rough-and-ready rule to distinguish between hypogynous, perigynous, and epigynous flowers is the following: If the stamens arise immediately beneath the ovary the flower is hypogynous, if the stamens arise from the top of the ovary the flower is epigynous, whilst if the stamens arise without contact with the ovary the flower is perigynous.

When all these points have been mastered, the student should examine with thoroughness a flower in which the perigynous condition is well marked.

We may take as our fourth example the flower of the Wild Rose, the fruits of which give us the beautiful red *hips* in autumn. The receptacle in this flower is cup-shaped, and assumes a red colour in late summer. From the rim of the red cup the sepals, petals, and stamens arise, whilst the carpels are formed at the bottom of the cup. The Wild Rose therefore belongs to the type shown diagrammatically in fig. 7, *c*.

As much practice as possible should be carried out in separating flowers into their component parts. The following questions should be answered in the case of each flower under examination:—

1. What are the number of sepals, petals, stamens, and carpels?
2. Do parts show union with like parts, e.g. petal with petal?
3. Do parts show union with unlike parts, e.g. petal with stamen?
4. Is the ovary superior or inferior?
5. Is the flower hypogynous, perigynous, or epigynous?

THE CLASSIFICATION OF PLANTS

Plants arrange themselves naturally into groups or families, all the members included in any one family bearing a close resemblance to one another. Thus a very superficial examination will show that the Broom is similar to the Laburnum in so far as the flowers are concerned. If these flowers be examined minutely they will be found to show many points of resemblance, and the same is true of the flowers of all the plants that have been included in the same family as the Broom and the Laburnum. In the same way the different families may be segregated into groups of families, each group being composed of families that resemble one another more closely than they do other families not included in the same group. To illustrate the above points we may again mention the Broom family, which is known as LEGUMINOSÆ. The various members—Gorse, Clover, Lupin, Pea, Bean, &c.—possess flowers so obviously alike in structure that their close relationship is obvious after a very superficial examination. In the same manner the Hemlock, Caraway, Fools' Parsley, Hogweed, &c. show equally great resemblances among themselves, and are included in the family UMBELLIFERÆ. A third example may be taken from the Daisy family, namely the COMPOSITÆ, which includes the Dandelion, Coltsfoot, Groundsel, Hawkweed, and a host of other flowers, all of which bear the same family stamp. When we now compare the LEGUMINOSÆ, UMBELLIFERÆ, COMPOSITÆ and the other families among themselves, we find for example that the Buttercup family (RANUNCULACEÆ) is more or less closely connected with the Poppy family (PAPAVERACEÆ), but is far removed from the COMPOSITÆ. The latter, on the other hand, is closely connected with the Teazel family (DIPSACEÆ). Inasmuch, therefore, as plants do not form a heterogeneous mass of discrete elements, it is obviously a matter of great convenience to be able to place a plant in its position in a scheme of classification, for when this is done we know not only the points of structure which we have discovered for ourselves, but also many other points which are found in all the members of a particular family. This mode of procedure may often serve a practical purpose. Thus the poisonous root of the Aconite (Monkshood) is sufficiently similar to the nutritious root of the Horse Radish (see fig. 8) to have caused mistakes—frequently fatal—by the substituting of the one for the other. If the flowers or fruit of these plants are present, the collector can at once ascertain whether he is gathering the right root, as the Horse Radish belongs to a family (CRUCIFERÆ) the flowers and fruit of which are quite different from those of the Aconite (RANUNCULACEÆ).

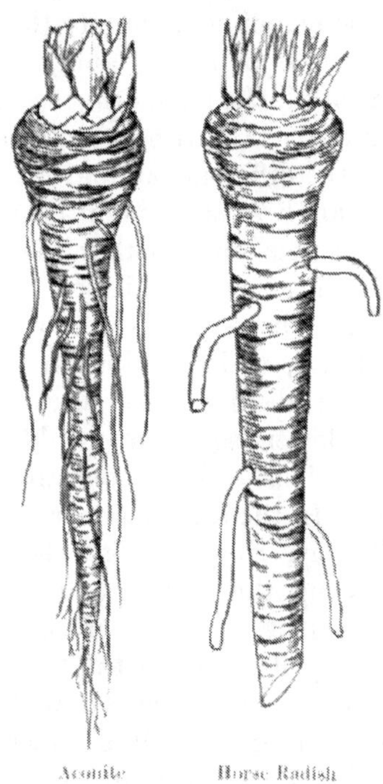

Fig. 8

Again, if further justification be necessary, attention to the classification of plants not only conduces to the methodical arrangement of the matter which the mind has gathered together, but also effects a simplification which considerably eases the study of the subject.

We may now therefore explain the chief subdivisions of the plant kingdom.

The higher flowering plants are divided into two great classes:—

I. **Monocotyledons.**
II. **Dicotyledons.**

The student should first determine to which of these two classes any particular plant belongs.

The Monocotyledons have their flower-parts arranged in threes (or sixes), e.g. the Lily flower is made up of 3 sepals, 3 petals, 6 stamens, and 3 carpels.

The Dicotyledons have flowers arranged in twos or threes or fives, e.g. the Primrose is made up of 5 sepals, 5 petals, and 5 stamens.

Having assigned a plant to one or other of these two classes, a further necessary step is to ascertain the Natural Order to which it belongs. If the plant belongs to the Monocotyledons, reference must be made to Table I, page 12. If it, on the other hand, is a Dicotyledon, its Natural Order will be found in one or other of Tables II, III, or IV. To ascertain which of these three to look up, the petals must be examined.

If absent, refer to Table II, page 12.
If present and free, refer to Table III, page 96.
If present and fused, refer to Table IV, page 151.

TABLE I.—MONOCOTYLEDO

Monocotyledons.
- Plants with petaloid flowers.
  - Superior ovary.
    - Water plant.
      - C
      - N
      - I
    - Land plant.
      - C
      - I
      - F
  - Inferior ovary.
    - Regular flowers,
    - Regular flowers,
    - Irregular flower
- Plants with petals absent or very inconspicuous.
  - Aquatic plants.
    - Float
    - Aqua
  - Land plants.
    - Stem
    - Stem

TABLE II.—DICOTYLEDON

Incompletæ (petals absent).
- No catkins.
  - Herbs with acrid milky juice. Ovary 3-celled. EUPHOR
  - Ovary 1–2-celled. URTICACEÆ.
  - Leaves with sheathing stipules. POLYG
  - Minute greenish flowers with no stipules.
- Catkins.
  - Male only in catkins. CUPULIFERÆ.
  - Male and female in catkins.
    - Male and
    - Male and

THE CLASSIFICATION OF POISONS

A poison has been defined as anything—apart from heat or electricity—which is capable of destroying life by absorption into the living system.

When a poison enters the system it may act on all the tissues with which it comes in contact, or it may pass into the circulation and act on organs more or less remote from the point of entry. So far as the vegetable poisons are concerned, they may be divided into four groups as follows:—

1. *Irritants*, e.g. Colchicum and Squill.
2. *Narcotic*, (*a*) Somniferous, e.g. Opium.
   (*b*) Deliriant, e.g. Belladonna.
   (*c*) Inebriant, e.g. Indian Hemp.
3. *Sedative*, (*a*) Cardiac, e.g. Digitalis.
   (*b*) Cerebral, e.g. Prussic Acid.
   (*c*) Neural, e.g. Aconite.
4. *Excito-motory*, e.g. Strychnia.

An *Irritant* produces irritation or excitement of any muscle, nerve, or other organ of the body; thus Colchicum poisoning produces vomiting, violent diarrhœa, gastric burning, abdominal pains, &c. as results of the irritation set up in various organs.

A *Narcotic* is a substance which produces sleep or torpor. Opium, for example, induces drowsiness, ending in profound insensibility. In the later stages of Opium poisoning the muscles become relaxed and the pulse very weak. In Belladonna poisoning the victim becomes delirious, whilst in poisoning from the drug which is used by the natives of the Malay Peninsula, namely Indian Hemp (*Cannabis indica*), giddiness, drowsiness, and a sensation of going mad are experienced.

A *Sedative* is a drug which allays irritation and assuages pain. The effect of Digitalis is to slow down the beating of the heart, producing a feeling of faintness and drowsiness. Prussic acid produces unconsciousness and loss of muscular power; these and other symptoms are the result of the operation of the poison on the nervous system. The effect of Aconite is to produce a feeling of numbness over the body and limbs, a sensation of burning in the throat, nausea, giddiness, loss of the power of speech, and unconsciousness.

Of the *Excito-motory* poisons Strychnia is the best example. The absorption of the poison is shown by the twitching of the muscles of the neck, body, and limbs, but there is retention of the senses.

Most of the poisons cited above, although so deadly in their operations, are among the most valuable of our medicines. This shows us that the difference between a medicine and a poison is a matter of degree, not of kind. Under one set of circumstances the absorption of a drug may result in beneficial, in other circumstances in injurious results. Again, whilst a certain dose may be beneficial under certain circumstances, the doubling of it may produce fatal effects. All drugs should be regarded as poisons, and the only distinction that should be made is between poisons that have, and those that have not, been harnessed to minister to the wants of man.

CHAPTER II

THE PHYSIOLOGY OF PLANT-LIFE: BEARING ON FORMATION OF DRUGS AND POISONS

The central feature in the physiology of a green plant is its power of capturing the energy contained in sunlight, and of utilizing it to build up various complex substances ultimately culminating in the formation of living matter or *protoplasm.* The *chlorophyll* or green colouring matter of plants arrests certain components of the light which shines on it, and with the aid of the energy thus obtained the protoplasm converts water and carbonic acid into *sugar.* The carbonic acid is derived from the store which is always present in the atmosphere, as a result of which there is invariably a certain amount of carbonic acid in solution in the water which passes into the plant. The formation of sugar, however, is only the first step. More raw materials are now utilized, mainly from the soil in the form of phosphates, nitrates, sulphates, &c. From these and the sugar the plant builds up complicated nitrogenous organic bodies called *proteins.* These all contain carbon, hydrogen, oxygen, and nitrogen; some contain sulphur and phosphorus, and a few iron. They compose a large part of the constituents of vegetable cells. They have not yet been obtained in a pure form, and the very simplest of them has a complex structure. Their association with protoplasm is very close, and it seems probable that the formation of this substance, which is the physical basis of life, is the culmination of a series of changes of a very complicated nature in the framework of the proteins. However formed, it is certain that the formation of protoplasm is accomplished by the expenditure of energy on the raw materials derived from the air and from the soil; and that when formed there is stored in the protoplasmic molecule a large quantity of energy. Under appropriate conditions this energy is liberated and work accomplished. The work here takes the form of growth, movement, and other manifestations which necessitate the expenditure of energy for their accomplishment. The whole process whereby this energy is liberated is called *respiration*, and in essentials is the same in the plant as in the animal. With the exception of one or two special cases, *oxygen* is necessary for the proper fulfilment of the process, and the liberation of energy is attended by a splitting up of the protoplasmic molecule, or of substances, whether protein or otherwise, which have been built up by the plant, into simpler components. It seems as though oxygen played the rôle of the match to the gunpowder. Now no two plants are alike in the nature of the substances which are formed as a result of these breaking-down processes; although it is true that in all of them carbonic acid is ultimately formed. The routes by which they reach the ground are very varied. It is interesting, however, to note that members which have been put into the same family on structural grounds often exhibit the same kind of end-products, showing that there is a relationship in function as well as in structure. Thus *bitterness* is the prevailing characteristic of the plants which compose the Compositæ; irritant poisons are common among the members of the Ranunculaceæ; *astringent* plants prevail in the Gentianaceæ.

Of course, in the present state of our knowledge it is not possible to explain all the chemical and physical changes which intervene before all comes to a stop and end-products are formed; we can only indicate the general trend, and study more carefully the stable products which are found at the end, and which undergo no further change. The number of substances thus formed is enormous, for, as already stated, every plant has its own way of carrying on the work of decomposition. We may classify them into four great groups:—

1. The *Waste-products*. These are of no further use to the plant, and are usually packed away in some form in which they will be out of the way. If they constitute a source of danger, they are first of all transformed into harmless substances.
2. The *Reserve products*. These are intended to be used up as food on a future occasion.
3. *End-products of definite use to the plant.* These undergo no further change, but, unlike the waste-products, the plant is benefited by their presence.
4. *Intermediate products of metabolism.*

For our purpose the waste- and other end-products are of chief interest.

Among the vegetable waste-products there occur numerous crystalline—and a few liquid—basic, nitrogenous substances called *alkaloids*, marked by the possession of very strong physiological action. *Morphine* was the first of these to be extracted; then followed the extraction of *strychnine, brucine, quinine*, &c. At present the number of alkaloids isolated and experimented with is very large, and chemists are, legitimately, very proud of having been able to accomplish the artificial production of some of them. The alkaloids vary considerably in nature: they are all poisonous, but small doses of a poison under certain circumstances become medicinal. Some plants containing alkaloids are therefore regarded as medicinal because a certain use has been found for their alkaloids; those that contain alkaloids for which no use has been found are merely *poisonous* plants. The difference is one of degree, not of kind.

Other plants contain alkaloids which, though poisonous, exert in small quantities a stimulating effect of a pleasant nature. Such, for example, are the *theobromine* of the cocoa plant and the *theïne* of the tea plant.

From the point of view of the plant economy it must be noted that alkaloids are waste-products and of no further use to the plant; their formation was, as it were, unavoidable, and they are to be regarded as by-products of processes of great importance to the plant.

Some plants are valuable because of the *aromatic substances* which they produce. These, again, are mainly by-products of important processes. Thus when *glucosides* are split up by ferments the sugar *glucose* is invariably formed. The production of glucose is an important operation, for the plant utilizes it as food material, but other substances are also formed, each glucoside producing one or two other substances as well. Among the latter are many aromatic substances, the presence of which brings the plants containing them into the category of medicinal or poisonous plants. Thus prussic acid is formed by the splitting up of the glucoside amygdalin; tannic acid is formed by the splitting up of the glucoside tannin. As similar by-products we may regard the commoner aromatic acids such as benzoic acid, cinnamic acid, gallic acid, and salicylic acid.

Again, the *resins* are substances which are always to be found in plants, and in all parts of them. They are semi-solid plant secretions, being found either as emulsions or oleo-resinous juices. When mixed with ethereal oils and aromatic acids they are called *balsams*; when mixed with gums and ethereal oils they are called *gum resins*. All these are waste-products, although in some plants they, accidentally as it were, play an important rôle by warding off from the plant the attacks of micro-organisms.

Another class of substances appearing as end-products are the *ethereal oils*, which are present in greater or less extent in all parts of flowering plants; the odours of plants are due to the volatile oils which they contain, and which are of great service in attracting insects to visit the flowers. Oil of cinnamon and oil of bitter almonds are two examples of this class of end-products. Oil of cloves, camphor, coumarin are other examples.

Among the *reserve matters* must be reckoned the *oils* and *fats* that are used in commerce. All of these, of plant origin, are derived from the seeds and fruits of various plants, the reason for their occurrence in these organs being obviously connected with the rôle which they play in supplying the germinating embryo of the plant with food. In the Linseed plant the reserve food material of its seed is principally oil, this substance taking the place of starch, which is commonly the principal reserve food in most plants. The same applies to other seeds used in commerce, e.g. those which supply us with oil of mustard, cotton-seed oil, rape oil, &c.

We must finally deal with an aspect in the physiology of plant-life which it is important for us to consider. As has just been shown, the activities of a plant are very complicated and very varied. They are also devoid of perfect constancy, and so the amount of the active principle in any plant, for the sake of which the plant is gathered, may show considerable variation. Many factors may contribute to this variation, such as soil, climate, or altitude, and in the cultivation of medicinal plants the possibility of such variations must be borne in mind. It is not possible to tell beforehand in which direction the variation is going to set. This can only be found by experiment; and the want of this knowledge is a severe handicap to a country desirous of growing certain medicinal plants, and entering into commercial rivalry with other nations which possess this knowledge. In Hungary, for example, experimental farms, to determine the nature of the conditions of growth of valuable medicinal plants, have been established for a long time. It is certain that the haphazard cultivation of wild plants, be they ever so valuable, will not succeed in the long run against the efforts of formidable organizations from abroad. We must recognize the existence of, and be able to cope with, the difficulties resulting from the physiological variations that may arise, when any particular plant is cultivated under different conditions.

CHAPTER III

MONOCOTYLEDONS

Liliaceæ.—This order is easily identified by the following:—

1. Parts of the flower in threes.
2. Conspicuous corolla.
3. Six stamens.
4. Superior ovary.

MEADOW SAFFRON (*Colchicum autumnale*).—This plant is easily the most important of the Monocotyledons, because the active principles contained in it are not only very poisonous, but also very valuable when harnessed to the service of man.

The flower is rose-coloured, comes up in autumn, and resembles the Crocus in its general appearance (fig. 9). It is hence often called *Autumn Crocus*. The stem takes the form of a *corm* (see fig. 9) about the size of a chestnut, is somewhat conical, flattened on one side, round on the other. The outer coat is brown, thin, and membranous, the inner reddish-yellow. When cut, a milky juice of a disagreeable odour and bitter taste exudes from the corm.

Fig. 9.—Meadow Saffron (*Colchicum autumnale*)

Poisonous Properties.—All parts are dangerous. Water in which the leaves and flowers have been allowed to stand becomes very poisonous. Cattle have been poisoned by eating the flowers along with the grass in the autumn months, and by eating the leaves from May to September. It is recorded that a woman, who, under the impression that they were onions, had picked up some bulbs of Colchicum thrown away by a tradesman in Covent Garden, died immediately after eating them. In 1862 a conviction of murder was obtained against a woman who had administered the drug of Colchicum to her victim. The active principle is an alkaloid called *colchicine*, which produces nausea, vomiting, and the other effects of a strong irritant poison. It is present in seeds to the extent of about 0·6 per cent.

Medicinal Properties.—Colchicine is regarded almost as a specific in acute attacks of gout, and is extensively employed in all forms of this malady.

Distribution.—The plant is found throughout Europe, and is fairly abundant in this country in moist meadows and pastures, though very local in character. It seems to thrive best in the West of England and in those counties which have an oolitic soil.

Collection.—The corms should be dug up in summer, peeled, sliced, and then dried. To collect the seeds, the capsule containing them must be cut off from the plant before it has opened, and hung up in a dry place inside muslin bags until the seeds are dry; the latter must not be washed.

Present Source of Supply.—Before the War the seeds were imported chiefly from France and Germany, the price of seeds in 1913 being 70*s.* per cwt., or about 7*d.* a lb. Now they cost 5*s.* a lb. Similarly the corms, chiefly from Germany, cost 38*s.* a cwt., or roughly 4*d.* a lb. Now they cost 4*s.* 6*d.* a lb. About 1 ton of Colchicum seed and 2–4 tons of Colchicum corms were imported annually into this country before the War.

Cultivation.—The young corm begins life about June as a small bud growing out of the parent corm. This grows up out of the ground and forms a flower in autumn. Several buds may appear from one corm, and so several plants are formed. When the plant is fully formed its basal part gradually expands to form a new corm. In this way several fresh corms are derived from the single parent. When the daughter-corms are sufficiently large, they may be separated from the remains of the parent corm and planted afresh.

LILY OF THE VALLEY (*Convallaria majalis*).—It is not necessary to give a detailed description of this well-known little Liliaceous white-flowered plant.

Poisonous Properties.—It is important to caution children against putting the flowers into their mouths as they sometimes do, for these are very poisonous on account of the presence in them of two glucosides called *convallamarin* and *convallarin*; the former acts upon the heart, the latter is purgative. The red berries of this plant are very attractive in appearance, and consequently a source of danger to children. Fortunately the berries are not often formed.

Medicinal Properties.—This plant is used as a substitute for Foxglove, as one of its active principles acts on the heart.

Distribution.—Found wild and in abundance in Lincolnshire, Derbyshire, Westmorland, and other counties.

Collection.—The flowers only are used, these being dried on the stalks. They are not worth collecting, except when very abundant. The flowers are gathered before the petals open to their full extent.

HERB PARIS (*Paris quadrifolia*).—This is not an important plant, as it has no medicinal properties and is not very common. It must be included in our list, however, because of its poisonous nature. When once noted the plant is easily recognized by the peculiarity of having four leaves spread out at the top of the stem, from the centre of which arises a large *green* flower (fig. 10). The whole plant is about a foot high. It is poisonous in

Fig. 10.—Herb Paris (*Paris quadrifolia*)

all its parts, and the berries which it forms are particularly so.

BLUEBELL OR WILD HYACINTH (*Scilla nutans*).—This familiar flower is gathered in great quantities by children. The whole plant, and particularly its underground part (corm), is of a poisonous nature, but as its active principles are very acrid there is little inducement to the child to swallow any of the parts.

THE HELLEBORES.—Care must be taken to distinguish the various Hellebores. We have:—

1. GREEN HELLEBORE (*Veratrum viride*), an American plant.
2. *Helleborus viridis* (also called GREEN HELLEBORE), a European plant belonging to the Buttercup family.
3. WHITE HELLEBORE (*Veratrum album*), a plant chiefly grown in Germany, and almost identical with the American Green Hellebore, but lacking in one of the principles (*cevadine*) which is present in the American species.
4. BLACK HELLEBORE (*Veratrum nigrum*), a native of Central and Southern Europe, but grown in our gardens.

The second of these will be mentioned later in its proper place; the others are Liliaceous plants, all characterized by the possession of greenish-white or purplish flowers, and oval-ribbed leaves similar to those of the Broad-leaved Plantain. These characters, combined with those common to all the Liliaceæ, make them readily distinguishable. All are poisonous plants, but their acrid taste acts as a sufficient deterrent to animals. There are many varieties in our gardens. Their cultivation for medicinal purposes in this country would not be a practicable project.

Among other poisonous members of the Liliaceæ which are either indigenous or are common garden plants are the CROWN IMPERIAL (*Fritillaria imperialis*), the SNAKE'S HEAD FRITILLARY (*Fritillaria Meleagris*), and the yellow-flowered TULIP (*Tulipa sylvestris*). They are fortunately very distasteful to the palate. They have no medicinal value.

Aroideæ.—This family is represented by several foreign poisonous plants, but in this country the sole representative is Lords-and-Ladies (*Arum maculatum*). A glance at fig. 11 will facilitate the identification of this species. The centre column is called a *spadix*, and on it are inserted the flowers. At the base are a number of flowers

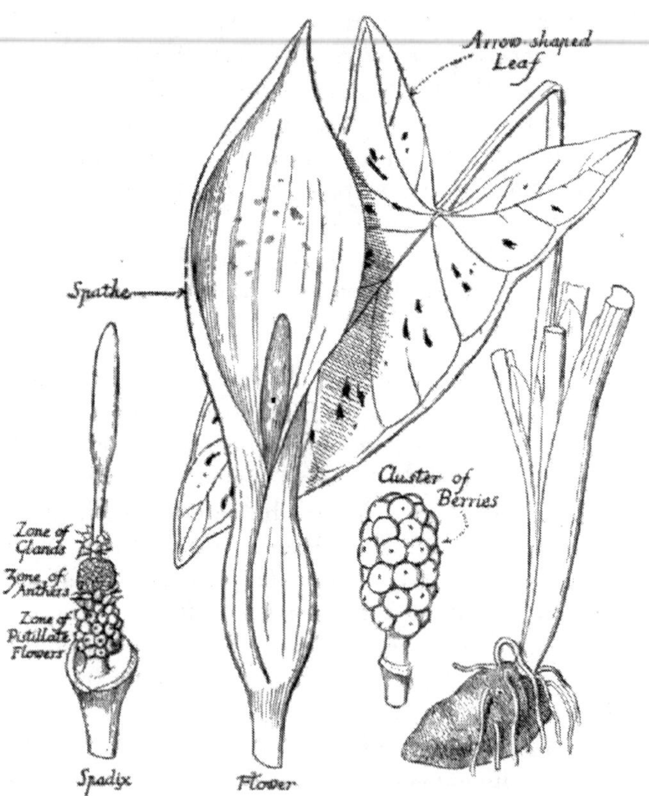

Fig. 11.—Lords-and-Ladies (*Arum maculatum*)

each consisting of a pistil only. Above this zone are a number of flowers each consisting of a purplish anther. Above the anthers is a ring of glands terminating in short threads. The spadix is then prolonged into a purple club-like extremity. Enveloping the whole is a relatively large leafy structure called the *spathe.* If further marks for identification are necessary, they are supplied by the arrow-shaped leaves of this plant. In autumn the pistil zone of flowers form a cluster of bright-scarlet berries of a very attractive appearance. In spite of their intensely acrid taste, the berries of this plant are sometimes eaten by children, with highly injurious results. A single drop of the juice will cause a burning sensation in the mouth and throat for hours afterwards. The roots, however, when properly prepared are wholesome and nutritious, and formerly the plant was cultivated for the sake of the starch that was got from the roots, the product being known as *Portland sago.* This could be used as food, as the poisonous properties common to all parts of this plant, being very volatile, disappeared during the process of drying. The roots contain not only starch, but sugar, gum, resin, albumen, and fat. It is interesting to note that an old name for this plant was *Starchwort;* it was used for stiffening the ruffs and frills worn by gentlemen and ladies in the reign of Queen Elizabeth.

SWEET FLAG or SWEET SEDGE (*Acorus Calamus*).—Belonging to the same family as the Cuckoo-Pint is a plant which was originally an inhabitant of eastern Europe but has now become established as a wild plant in England, being found on the edges of lakes and streams. This is the Sweet Flag (fig. 12), the rhizome of which possesses important medicinal properties. In Germany and Holland the plant is cultivated for the market. It is found in watery places, and is easily distinguished from all other British plants by its erect sword-shaped leaf, 2–3 feet long, and numerous stalkless primitive flowers, crowded on a fleshy structure called the *spadix.* All the parts of the plants are very fragrant. The underground stem (rhizome) is esteemed as a valuable medicine in India, and for many years was imported into Great Britain from this country. The value of the rhizome depends on the presence of an aromatic volatile oil (2·8 per cent) and a bitter principle called *acorin*. The drug

Fig. 12.—Sweet Flag (*Acorus Calamus*)

has certain tonic and stimulant properties, and has been used for dyspepsia, ague, &c.

Cultivation.—Grows readily on unused ground in damp localities near ditches and streams. There is a ready sale for the dried rhizomes, the War being responsible for the increased demand.

Gramineæ.—The general appearance of the grasses is familiar to everyone, and no attempt need be made to particularize their characteristics. Of the British grasses there is only one which has medicinal properties of any importance.

COUCH-GRASS (*Agropyron repens*).—We used to import, chiefly from Germany, 4–5 tons of this plant per annum. Its price has gone up from 25s. a cwt. to 50s. a cwt. At present our supplies are home-grown, but the quality is poor. The Couch-grass is recognized by the following characteristics:—

1. Flat leaves with short hairs on ribs of upper surface.
2. Flower-bearing stalks elongated.
3. Flower-groups arranged on a *zigzag* central stalk (fig. 13).
4. Plant extends 1–4 feet above the ground.
5. Underground stem $\frac{1}{12}$ inch in diameter and of a dark straw colour; it bears 5–6 prominent longitudinal ridges.

The underground stem contains a substance called *triticin* (a carbohydrate), as well as certain sugars.

Medicinal Properties.—Couch-grass has been employed as a diuretic in certain affections of the bladder.

Distribution.—Very common in our hedges and fields, where it is exceedingly difficult to exterminate it. The underground stems (*suckers*) of the Couch-grass are arranged in short segments like a bamboo cane or a drain-pipe, and a single segment if left in the ground can reproduce the whole plant.

Collection.—It is the underground segmented suckers that are used in medicine.

Cultivation.—It will be apparent from what has been stated that there should be no difficulty in cultivating this plant. Our present supply, drawn from our native growths, is of poor quality. It will therefore be neces sary to improve the physiological qualities of our own

Fig. 13.—Couch Grass (*Agropyron repens*)

products by careful cultivation if we desire to be inde pendent of foreign supplies.

Amaryllidaceæ and **Dioscoreaceæ.**—These two orders differ from Liliaceæ in having an *inferior* instead of a superior ovary. They are similar in possessing 6 stamens, in addition to the other characters peculiar to Monocotyledons.

Black Bryony (*Tamus communis*).—This species, which is unknown in Scotland and Ireland, is the only British representative of a family (Dioscoreaceæ) possessing many foreign representatives, the best known of which is the Yam plant. It is recognized by its climbing habits, its tendency to scramble over hedges, and its oval, pointed, and glossy leaves (fig. 14). The flowers are small, green, and *unisexual*; that is, the stamens and carpels are never found together in the same flower, some flowers being carpellary only, others staminate only. The large fleshy root is sometimes used in its fresh state as an external application to bruises, and taken internally it acts as an emetic. In the Middle Ages these roots were accredited with healing virtues, and were supposed to be especially good for rheumatism.

Care must be taken to distinguish the Black Bryony from Black-berried Bryony (*Bryonia alba*) and Red-berried Bryonia (*Bryonia dioica*). The two latter are not Monocotyledons and have nothing in common with Black Bryony.

Black Bryony has a very acrid root and is used by quacks as a purgative; but the remedy may be found to be worse than the disease, and consequently emphasis should be laid on the poisonous rather than on the medicinal qualities of this plant. It may be noted further that the berries have been known to cause paralysis of the lower limbs.

Black Bryony root is listed as a plant which is worth collecting, owing to its being in demand by herbalists. It is sold in the fresh state, and is kept in damp sand. The root is in the best condition for collecting in April.

With regard to the Amaryllidaceæ, this order may be dismissed in a few words. The bulbs of the Daffodil are powerfully emetic, and the flowers also must be

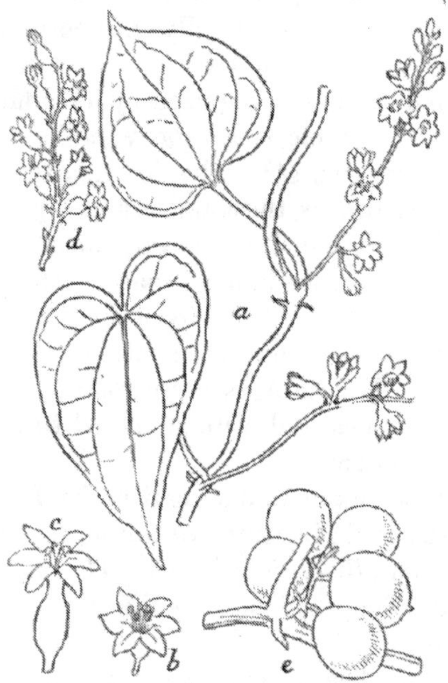

Fig. 14.—Black Bryony (*Tamus communis*)

a, Branch with cordate leaves (net-veined). *b*, Staminate flower. *c*, Pistillate flower. *d*, Raceme of pistillate flowers. *e*, Cluster of ripe berries (poisonous)

regarded with suspicion. The odour of the Poet's Narcissus (*Narcissus poeticus*) has been known to cause headache and vomiting, and the bulbs of this plant are even more dèleterious than those of the Daffodil.

Iridaceæ.—The possession of *three* stamens and an inferior ovary are the distinguishing marks of this order. All the members have sheathing leaves and showy flowers.

Yellow Flag or Corn Flag (*Iris Pseud-acorus*).—This stout aquatic plant has sword-shaped leaves about 2–3 feet long. The yellow flowers are very conspicuous objects in marshes and on the banks of rivers, and when once seen are easily recognized again. It must be noted that the three styles are yellow like the rest of the flower, and look like petals (fig. 15).

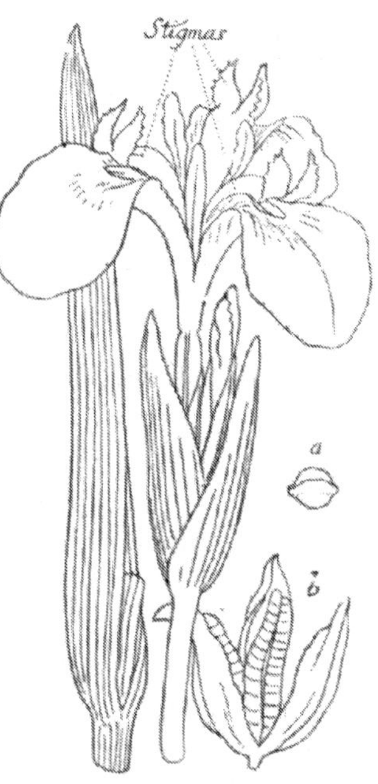

Fig. 15.—Yellow Flag or Corn Flag (*Iris Pseud-acorus*)

a, Seed. *b*, Capsule opening with seeds within.

Poisonous Properties.—Agriculturists should be made cognizant of the poisonous qualities of this plant, as it constitutes a danger to cattle. The flowers and the underground stem (rhizome) have marked emetic effects on cattle, and apparently there is nothing sufficiently distasteful in the plant to restrain them from eating it. The rhizome when fresh is very acid and very astringent; after drying the acidity disappears, but the astringency remains. The rhizome yields a good black dye when treated with sulphate of iron. In addition, the seeds are used as a substitute for coffee.

Stinking Iris.—Belonging to the same genus as the last is the Stinking Iris or Gladwin (*Iris fœtidissima*), a plant which is common in the hedges of limestone and chalky districts, especially in the South of England. It is somewhat like the last but smaller, and the flowers are of a dull leaden hue. The leaves are so acrid that they produce a burning taste when put into the mouth: the whole plant when bruised emits a very disagreeable odour; the berries are of a beautiful orange-scarlet colour.

There is a market among herbalists for the roots of this plant; they are collected in March.

SAFFRON CROCUS (*Crocus sativus*).—This plant is said to be naturalized at Saffron Walden in Essex, where it is largely cultivated. The flowers which come up in autumn are purplish-violet in colour, and possess the general characters of the ordinary garden Crocus. It is especially characterized by having a long, pale-yellow style terminating in three deep-red elongated stigmas. These protrude from the flower.

Fig. 16.—Stigmas of *Crocus sativus*

Medicinal Properties. — The stigmas alone possess any medicinal value (fig. 16). Each stigma is about an inch long, and tubular in shape. From the stigmas, about 1 per cent of *volatile oil*, also a red colouring matter called *crocin*, and a bitter principle called *picrocrocin* are obtained. The drug is employed as a colouring agent and as a stimulant, an antispasmodic, and as an emmenagogue.

Distribution.—The uses of Saffron have been known for many centuries, so that it is not possible to say where the plant is indigenous.

Present Source of Supply.—Most of the European supply is exported from Spain.

The following table will, it is hoped, prove useful to the student in reviewing the poisonous and medicinal Monocotyledons mentioned in the text:—

	Outstanding Characteristics of Order.	Outstanding Characteristi
Liliaceæ..........	Superior ovary, 6 stamens.	1. AUTUMNAL CROCUS. Rose-colo in autumn.
		2. LILY OF THE VALLEY. White,
		3. HERB PARIS. Plant with 4 le rises a large green flower.
		4. WILD HYACINTH. Blue-petalle
		5. HELLEBORE. Greenish-white o
		6. FRITILLARY. Chequered flower
		7. YELLOW-FLOWERED TULIP.
Aroideæ..........	Groups of stalkless primitive flowers attached to a central column.	8. LORDS-AND-LADIES. Arrow-sl fig. 11; scarlet berries.
		9. SWEET FLAG or SWEET SED numerous stalkless flowers
Gramineæ.......		10. COUCH-GRASS.
Dioscoreaceæ...	Inferior ovary, 6 stamens.	11. BLACK BRYONY. Climbing hab oval, pointed, and glossy le
Iridaceæ......	Inferior ovary, 3 stamens.	12. YELLOW FLAG or CORN FLAG flowers.
		13. STINKING IRIS. Flowers of di disagreeable odour when b
		14. SAFFRON CROCUS. Purple-viol red tubular stigmas.

CHAPTER IV

THE INCOMPLETÆ

In this division are grouped all those flowers in which the perianth is either wanting altogether or is present in only a rudimentary form. It follows, therefore, that the flowers of the majority of them are inconspicuous, and are practically unknown except to those who have made a study of botany. This fact renders the identification of the orders included in the Incompletæ somewhat difficult; but in spite of the defection of the flowers it will be found that each order has its characteristic features in regard to structure, habit, &c. If these features are known there should be no difficulty in identifying the order to which a particular specimen of the Incompletæ belongs.

Euphorbiaceæ.—The Spurge Family.

Distinguishing characteristics:—

1. Flowers not grouped in the pendulous collection called *catkins*.
2. Ovary three-celled.

In this country the order is represented by three genera:—

1. EUPHORBIA. The Spurges. All plants exuding an acrid milky juice.
2. BUXUS. The Box.
3. MERCURIALIS. The Dog's Mercury.

The whole family must be regarded with suspicion, for in some form or other an acrid, biting poison permeates the entire group. In tropical countries the deadliest poisons are found in members of the Euphorbiaceæ, e.g.

the MANCHINEEL TREE (*Hippomane Mancinella*) is said to inflict a fatal illness on persons who sleep beneath its shade; other members supply savages with their deadliest poisons. It is therefore scarcely a matter for surprise that the British representatives should possess in a milder form the same characteristics as their tropical relatives. The plants of this family are easily distinguished by their milky juice and by the peculiarity of the flowers. We

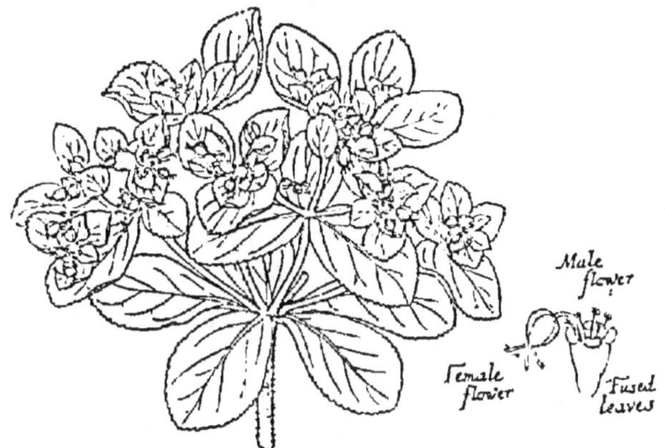

Fig 17.—Sun Spurge (*Euphorbia Helioscopia*)

may take the flower of the Sun Spurge as a typical example. What appears to be a single flower will be found on observation to be numerous male flowers, each consisting of a single stamen jointed to its pedicel (fig. 17), and arising from the axil of a small leaf at its base. In addition there is also a female flower consisting of a pistil made up of three fused carpels. The pistil is placed pendent at the end of a comparatively long stalk (fig. 17). This whole collection of one female and several male flowers is set inside a small cup-like structure, which is not a perianth, but rather a collection of small leaves which have fused to form the cup. Lastly, round the edge of the cup are five rounded glands. A glance at fig. 17 will make these points clear.

The milky exudations are the most poisonous structures of these plants. Of the thirteen species of Spurges in this country there are records against three of them, viz. the Sun Spurge, the Caper Spurge, and the Petty Spurge.

THE SUN SPURGE (*Euphorbia Helioscopia*).—The above description of the Spurge flower was taken from the flower as seen in the Sun Spurge. It is distinguished from the rest in possessing the following characteristics:—

1. The golden-green hue of its spreading umbel.
2. The umbel has several serrated leaves at its base.
3. The umbel is large in proportion to the rest of the plant.

Examine fig. 17 for verification of these points.

Other names are WART-WORT, CHURN-STAFF, CAT'S MILK. The first name is given because of the use of the milky juice to cure warts. It has also been improperly used to cure sore eyelids, causing, in many cases, needless pain to the sufferer. A boy is known to have died after eating the Sun Spurge. It was found that the mouth, throat, and stomach of the boy had become highly inflamed and corroded.

THE CAPER SPURGE (*Euphorbia Lathyris*).—This is a tall herbaceous plant some 2–4 feet high. It is readily distinguished from all other Spurges by its opposite leaves (fig. 18). It was originally a Continental species, but is now naturalized with us.

The unripe fruit is like that of the common garden Nasturtium (*Tropæolum majus*), and, like that fruit, it has been used for pickling purposes, hence its name of Caper Spurge. A fairly large amount of information has been collected concerning this plant. As is the case in all Euphorbias, the milky juice is acrid and poisonous. The seeds yield an oil which is violently purgative and speedily becomes rancid. The green pistil contains the acrid milky juice, the poison of which is stated to be neutralized when steeped in salt and water and then in vinegar. The poison being thus removed, the fruit can be used in a pickle like any other edible vegetable, but the danger is too great and the gain too small to make experiments in this direction desirable. On the Continent the peasants sometimes use the seeds of this plant as a purgative, but in many cases not without injurious effects, as, in addition to being a purgative, the poison acts as a strong irritant, causing internal and external painful blisters. The record against this species is a black one, children being the chief sufferers.

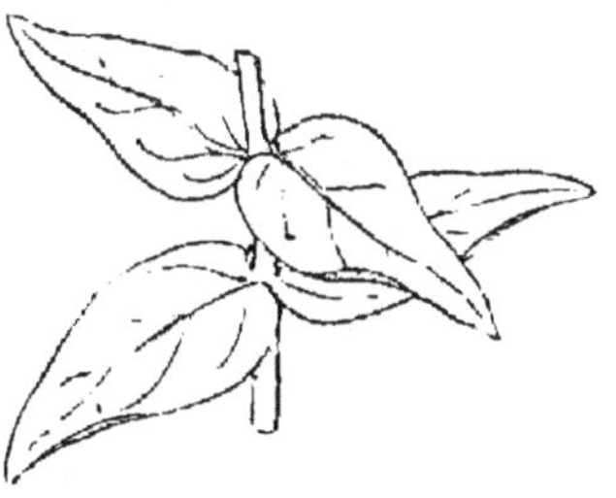

Fig 18.—Leaves of Caper Spurge (*Euphorbia Lathyris*)

THE PETTY SPURGE (*Euphorbia Peplus*).—A very common weed, distinguished by its pale hue: it reaches 6–10 inches from the ground. The umbel bearing the flowers *has only three rays*. It is known that, in one case at least, a boy has died of eating this plant.

In the case of the other species the fact of their having no records against them is in all probability mainly due to their not having been put to the same test. The seeds of members of this order are largely employed by quacks who profess to cure the ailments of ignorant folk. When taken internally their use is undoubtedly fraught with danger.

BOX (*Buxus sempervirens*).—At the present day the use of this plant as borders for garden paths and lawns has been largely discontinued, and its appearance on the grounds of a house usually indicates that the house in question has not been recently built.

Box can be recognized by the following characteristics:—

1. The flowers are white and have 4 stamens.
2. The plant is an evergreen shrub.
3. Except in Surrey, it is found only as a border for plots, paths, &c.
4. The leaves are oval, and have a small notch at the apex (see fig. 19).

Box is injurious to men and animals. It has been fraudulently used in place of hops in the making of beer because of its bitter taste, with disastrous consequences. It has also been used for the adulteration of Senna leaves. A case came within the experience of the writer, in which on one occasion several sheep died after eating Box leaves which had been given to them by a child.

Fig. 19.—Box Leaf

The poisonous principle is emetic and purgative. Fortunately, so far as man is concerned, the leaf is both bitter and nauseous to the human palate. In Persia, however, where this plant is abundant, camels will eat the leaves voraciously, with disastrous results; in fact, in some districts it is not possible to keep animals, on account of the abundance of the Box plant. It has been stated that the porcupine can eat the leaves and twigs with impunity. This is remarkable, if true, for even pigs are known to have succumbed after having eaten the plant.

MERCURY:—

DOG'S MERCURY (*Mercurialis perennis*).

ANNUAL MERCURY (*Mercurialis annua*).

In this country, Dog's Mercury is much more common

than Annual Mercury, although the latter is not infrequently met with as a garden plant. Dog's Mercury is

Fig. 20.—Dog's Mercury (*Mercurialis perennis*)

a, Male flower. *b*, Same, enlarged. *c*, Female flower.

common woodland herbaceous weed standing from to 12 inches high. It is somewhat difficult to identify rom the flowers, these being small and insignificant, and lso of the same colour as the leaves. The flowers are unisexual, which means that no single flower possesses both stamens and pistil. Further, the same plant bears only one kind of flower. We can therefore distinguish between male plants bearing stamens only and female plants bearing carpels only. It is easier to identify the plant from the leaves (see fig. 20). Each stem bears in the upper part several pairs of stalked, large, rough leaves of the shape shown in fig. 20. If the plant also bears a flower, this will consist, if a male flower, of a calyx of 3 sepals together with about 9 stamens; or if a female flower, of a calyx of 3 sepals enclosing a pistil of 2 fused carpels the styles of which are free.

For its identification, reliance must be placed chiefly on the peculiar appearance of the plant as a whole, the leaves being large for such a lowly plant, and the cluster of small green flowers having a distinctive character of their own (fig. 20). Again, many of the plants have *barren* flowers—that is, flowers devoid of stamens or carpels—and these grow on long stalks which arise from the uppermost leaves. These present characteristics which are readily recognized when looking for the plant.

On account of the disagreeable odour of Dog's Mercury animals very rarely eat it, but the plant has been known to prove fatal to sheep when given to them mixed with herbage. Within the writer's knowledge a case of litigation depended on proof being led as to whether certain horses had or had not eaten Dog's Mercury. When subjected to boiling or to drying the poison is rendered innocuous, and the leaves may be eaten by cattle with impunity; in fact, in certain parts of Germany the leaves are eaten as a vegetable, and in France they are boiled and then served to pigs. The seeds are dangerously purgative, and even fatal results are on record.

Annual Mercury (*Mercurialis annua*).—This is a familiar garden annual in some parts of the country.

It is sometimes known as Wild Spinach. It is distinguished from the preceding by its branched stems and its smooth smaller leaves of a light-green hue.

In some places it is boiled as a pot herb. Ray has recorded a case in which five persons suffered severely after eating this plant fried with bacon; and other cases are on record, in two of which death intervened one hour after eating this plant as a vegetable.

Among herbalists there is a market for Dog's Mercury: it is listed as one of the plants for which there is a ready sale in the British market.

Urticaceæ.—The Nettle Family. In this family are included:—

1. The Stinging Nettle.
2. The Hop.
3. Pellitory of the Wall.

As a family Urticaceæ is distinguished from the Euphorbiaceæ by the structure of the ovary, this organ having only one or two cells, whilst in the Euphorbiaceæ it always contains three compartments.

STINGING NETTLE:—

GREAT NETTLE (*Urtica dioica*). Leaves tapering to a point.

SMALL NETTLE (*Urtica urens*). Leaves elliptical.

The sting of the Nettle is too familiar to need a special description. When touched the delicate prickle is burst, and into the slight wound made in the skin a small exudation of formic acid takes place. The effect is purely local. After boiling, the plant is free from any deleterious substances, and is commonly boiled and eaten as a vegetable; in parts of Scotland the tips are made into a soup, and the nettle beer that is prepared in many localities is not only a palatable drink but also a cooling medicine.

HOP (*Humulus Lupulus*).—The Hop industry is an

important one in the South of England, the plant being cultivated for the sake of the substances which are contained in the *strobiles*, as the cone-like, leafy fruits are called. The odour peculiar to hops is due to a volatile oil, of which they contain 0·7 per cent. The bitterness of the Hop is due to a substance called *lupamaric acid*, and resides, like the oil, in the glands which are found at the base of the leaf-structures composing the cone. The volatile oil produces soporific and sedative effects, while the

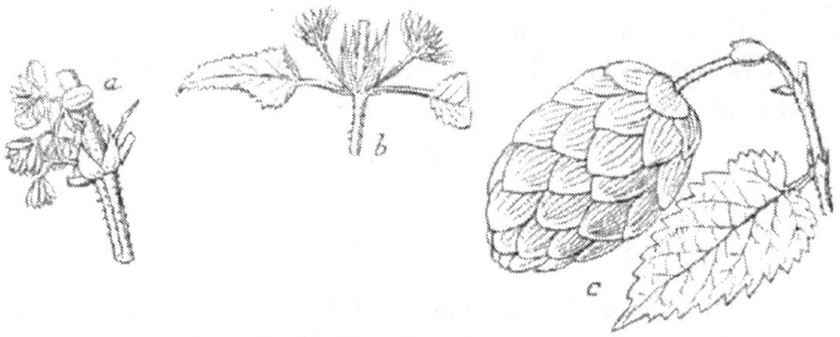

Fig. 21.—Hop (*Humulus Lupulus*)

a, Male flower. *b*, Female flower. *c*, Strobile.

lupamaric acid is stomachic and tonic. It is for this combination of properties that the cones are so much prized by the brewer. The strobilus is shown in fig. 21.

The young shoots of the Hop when boiled are said to make a delicious vegetable.

Pellitory of the Wall (*Parietaria officinalis*).—This is a herbaceous plant, characterized by the hairy flowers which grow in clusters in the axils of the leaves, and its reddish brittle stems. An infusion of this plant is a favourite medicine in some rural districts.

Polygonaceæ.—The Dock and Rhubarb Family.

The Polygonaceæ are all herbs, and are best distinguished by their *stipules*. A stipule is a leaf that is attached to another leaf. In the Polygonaceæ the stipule is very characteristic, as it is membranous and encircles the stalk on which it is borne. Again, the flowers are always *unisexual*, because each bears either stamens only or carpels only, never both together. The male or staminate flower consists of a perianth of 3–6 members, and there are usually 5–8 stamens. The female or carpellary flower has the same kind of perianth, and a pistil with either 2 or 3 styles (fig. 22). Further, the *fruit* differs from almost all others in having a *flattened* or *triangular* structure. Lastly, the inflorescence is an outstanding feature, for although the flowers are small there are plenty of them, and they crowd the stalk which rises erect above the rest of the plant.

Fig 22.—Diagram of Female Flower of Polygonaceæ

Speaking generally, care must be observed in dealing with this family, as there is apt to be a marked difference in the properties of the various parts. Thus the leaves and leaf-stalks are generally acid and astringent, and in some cases, as in the Rhubarb, agreeable to the taste, while the roots are nauseous and purgative. The fact that one part of the plant can be eaten with impunity furnishes no guarantee regarding the edibility of the other parts of the plant.

British Genera:—

1. Polygonum.—Fruit a flattened or triangular nut.
2. Rumex (Dock).—Fruit a triangular nut *covered by an enlarged inner perianth.*
3. Oxyria (Mountain Sorrel).

Rhubarb (*Rheum*).—The commercial drug known as Rhubarb is the rhizome of a species of Rheum which grows wild in North-West China and Eastern Tibet.

It is therefore quite different from the rhubarb grown in our gardens and does not concern us here. As a matter of fact, our culinary rhubarb is not a British species either, but as it has become as familiar as any other vegetable grown in our gardens, we may fairly accept its naturalization. Its source of origin has not yet been ascertained, and the views that have been advanced on this point need not detain us here. The plant has lately sprung into prominence, because, owing to the desire to make the utmost use of our green food, attention has been misdirected to the possibilities of rhubarb leaves. The following extract copied from the *Glasgow Herald* of 5th May, 1917, may be taken as an example of what has happened on several occasions: "An inquest was held at Pinner on Saturday on D—— P——, 12 years of age, who died as the result of eating cooked rhubarb leaves. Mrs. P—— said she followed the advice given in a newspaper. The evidence showed that in the family a mother and three daughters were taken ill after eating the leaves, but the others recovered. Mrs. P—— said she cooked the leaves like cabbage. A doctor who attended the girl said the symptoms were those of oxalic poisoning, and the results of the post-mortem confirmed this. The Coroner added a strong warning against eating rhubarb leaves, and said there were other cases of similar deaths."

The writer could match this account with at least a dozen others giving similar evidence of the baneful effects of eating the blades of rhubarb leaves. Two reasons have contributed to the large number of such accidents. In the first place, it is difficult to realize that whilst tons of the leaf-stalk are eaten every year, another part of the same plant organ, namely the leaf-blade, should be in any way dangerous; consequently many have been emboldened to make the venture. In the second place, several of the older writers, reliable in many respects, have spoken in praise of the culinary qualities of the rhubarb leaf-blade. With regard to the second point, we find in the famous *Herball* of Gerard the name of *Hippolapathum sativum* or Munkes *Rubarbe*, which he describes as a "holsome potherbe". This plant is not a Rhubarb but a Dock, and has been referred by experts to *Rumex Patienta*, a dock from Southern Europe. But the evil has been done in that the name "Rhubarb" has been associated with the term "holsome potherbe". Again, "Monk's rhubarb" appears in Syme's edition of *English Botany* for *Rumex alpinus*, which is also a Dock. It is not, therefore, surprising that the idea should be prevalent that rhubarb leaf-blades could be eaten with impunity.

With regard to the difference in the character of the stalk as compared with the leaf, the problem is one which can be settled by a consideration of the nature of the blade's activity. It has been stated that sugar is formed in the green parts of plants. Now in the multifarious activities which subsequently take place the production of oxalic acid is a feature in the metabolism of most, if not all, green plants. It may arise by the oxidation of the sugar that is formed in the leaf, or by the decomposition of the proteins. In the Rhubarb its formation is more abundant than in most other plants. Now, the presence of oxalic acid is a source of danger to the plant itself, and for that reason a plant does not thrive unless some substance like lime is presented to it to neutralize this oxalic acid, and cause the formation of a neutral substance like calcium oxalate. The last-named substance is carried away in solution. If the oxalic acid enters into combination, not with calcium, but with another somewhat similar substance, namely potassium, the formation of the highly poisonous binoxalate of potassium may take place. The essential points to note are the following:—

1. The production of oxalic acid in a relatively large quantity is an essential feature in the metabolism of the Rhubarb plant.
2. This production takes place mainly in the leaves, probably from the oxidation of sugar; consequently there will be a greater chance of finding free oxalic acid in the leaf than in parts further away.
3. The neutralization of oxalic axid is a paramount necessity to the plant, and this is accomplished before the product is carried away down the leaf-stalk.
4. A probable second source of danger is the fact that instead of calcium the neutralization may be accomplished through the agency of potassium, the compound of oxalic acid with the latter being highly poisonous. (The active principle in the poisonous *salts of lemon* is a compound of potassium and oxalic acid, namely binoxalate of potash.)

Finally, it may be noted that in boiling the plant with water containing baking or washing soda there is always a risk that chemical changes may take place, involving the removal of the calcium from its beneficent combination with oxalic acid, in which case poisonous results would follow, either from the acid itself or from the substance formed by its new alliance. Whatever the theoretical explanation may be, the fact remains, after many trials, that rhubarb leaf-blades are baneful in their effects, and that, except for a very few people, rhubarb leaf-stalks can be eaten not only with enjoyment but also with digestive profit.

THE POLYGONUM GROUP.—Distinguished from the

other genera by the perianth being composed of *five* parts.

SNAKEWEED or BISTORT (*Polygonum Bistorta*).—There is a sale for this plant owing to its root having tonic and astringent properties. It is found in moist meadows. It can be recognized by the following characteristics:—

1. The stem is erect, and 12–18 inches high.
2. The root is large and twisted.
3. The leaves are egg-shaped.

Fig. 23.—Curly or Yellow Dock (*Rumex crispus*)

In some parts of England BUCKWHEAT (*Polygonum Fagopyrum*) is cultivated as food for pheasants, who are very partial to it. On the Continent it is cultivated extensively to provide food for the humbler classes.

THE RUMEX GROUP (Dock). — Distinguished from the other genera of Polygonaceæ by the perianth being composed of *six* segments or parts.

The roots of CURLY or YELLOW DOCK (*Rumex crispus*) and of WATER or RED DOCK (*Rumex aquaticus*) are in request by the herbalist because of their astringent and tonic qualities. The first is common on fallow ground, and is recognized by its acute curled leaves (fig. 23). The second is found on river banks, and is recognized by its heart-shaped, entire perianth. It is somewhat like the Yellow Dock but is not so crisped.

Chenopodiaceæ.—The Goose-foot Family. This family does not demand a detailed description. One of its members, called GOOD KING HENRY, a plant of distinctive appearance often found near villages, is a good substitute for Spinach.

SUMMARY OF THE INCOMPLETÆ

We have above dealt only with four Natural Orders. These are the Euphorbiaceæ, the Urticaceæ, the Polygonaceæ, and the Chenopodiaceæ. The reader, as soon as he has satisfied himself that any particular plant under observation belongs to the Incompletæ, should review the outstanding features of each of these four orders. The following facts should be borne in mind:—

1. The *Spurges* exude a milky juice when bruised, and their ovary is three-celled.
2. The ovary of the *Urticaceæ* is only one- to two-celled.
3. The leaves of the *Polygonaceæ* have sheathing stipules at their base.
4. The *Chenopodiaceæ* have minute green flowers, no stipules at the base of the leaves, and the ovary possesses one cell and one ovule.

CHAPTER V

THE POLYPETALÆ

The Polypetalæ group comprises all those Dicotyledons the flowers of which possess free petals. In order to determine whether a plant belongs to this group it is only necessary—

1. To prove that it belongs to the Dicotyledons.
2. To ascertain that the petals of its flower are not joined.

The number both of poisonous and of medicinal plants in the Polypetalæ is very large.

Ranunculaceæ.—Buttercup Family. This is a very important family from our point of view, as owing to the fact that a poisonous, acrid, and narcotic principle prevails in varying degree throughout the order, there is scarcely one plant which can be regarded as harmless, while some are deadly.

The distinguishing marks of the order are:—

1. Free petals. 2. Numerous free stamens.
3. Free carpels (fig. 1)

Some members of the Rose family (Rosaceæ) also possess all three of these characteristics: but in this family all the flowers are perigynous, whilst in the Ranunculaceæ hypogyny prevails.

The number of distinctly poisonous plants is so large in the Ranunculaceæ that it is advisable to draw up a separate diagnostic table for its members.

Traveller's Joy (*Clematis Vitalba*).

Greenish-white flowers.

A hedge shrub.

Styles of carpels converted when ripe into long feathery tails.

WOOD ANEMONE (*Anemone nemorosa*).

White flower tinged with purple or pink.

Leaves appear *after* flower.

Carpels become tailless achenes like those of the Buttercup.

BUTTERCUP GROUP:—

1. FIELD BUTTERCUP (*Ranunculus acris*).

   Yellow flower *with round smooth stalk* (fig. 24, *a*).

2. BULBOUS CROWFOOT (*Ranunculus bulbosus*).

   Yellow flower with reflexed calyx and *furrowed* stem (fig. 24, *b*).

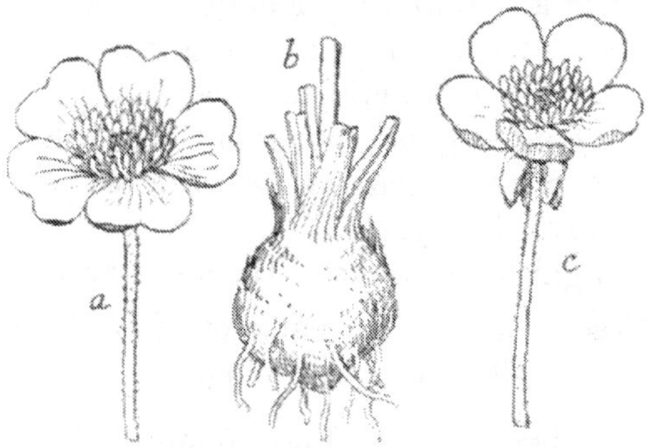

Fig. 24.—*a*, Field Buttercup. *b*, *c*, Root and Flower of Bulbous Crowfoot.

3. CREEPING CROWFOOT (*Ranunculus repens*).

   Yellow flower with *furrowed* stalk and *creeping* stem.

4. SPEARWORT (*Ranunculus Flammula*).

   Yellow flower half the size of Buttercup.

   Long, narrow, pointed leaves with a toothed margin (fig. 25).

   Grows in wet places.

   Stem lies flat on ground.

5. LESSER CELANDINE (*Ranunculus Ficaria*).

Yellow flower, corolla of 7 or 8 petals, and calyx of 3 sepals.

Heart-shaped leaves.

6. CELERY-LEAVED RANUNCULUS (*Ranunculus Sceleratus*).

Very small yellow flowers, part bearing achenes being relatively large and raised above rest of flower (fig. 26).

Grows in wet places.

7. WATER CROWFOOT (*Ranunculus aquatilis*).

White flower.

Floating leaves divided into three.

Leaves under water thread-like.

MARSH MARIGOLD (*Caltha palustris*).

Large golden-yellow flowers

Round leaves (fig. 27).

Grows in wet places.

HELLEBORE (HELLEBORUS).

a. GREEN HELLEBORE (*Helleborus viridis*).

b. FETID HELLEBORE (*Helleborus fœtidus*).

Eight to ten *tubular* petals.

Five large greenish persistent sepals.

In *a* the sepals are spreading.

In *b* the sepals are erect and overlapping.

c. BLACK HELLEBORE / CHRISTMAS ROSE } (*Helleborus niger*) (fig. 28).

Large white sepals.

Black underground stem (rhizome).

ACONITE, WOLFBANE (*Aconitum Napellus*).

Deeply divided leaves with tall spikes of blue to white flowers.

One sepal hood-shaped (fig. 29).

COLUMBINE (*Aquilegia vulgaris*).

Five coloured sepals.

Five petals.

Flower bears resemblance to five little birds putting their beaks together.

Compound leaves (fig. 30).

LARKSPUR (*Delphinium Ajacis*).

Coloured calyx, one sepal being prolonged into a spur.

Within spurred sepal are two spurred petals (fig. 31).

TRAVELLER'S JOY, OLD MAN'S BEARD (*Clematis Vitalba*).—Among the secrets which tramps possess is a method for raising sores on their arms by rubbing into skin abrasions the juice of Traveller's Joy. Sores are thereby raised which excite commiseration, and may lead to the dispensing of various material benefits, preferably in the form of coin of the realm. These gentry know that though the poison which causes the sore is acrid and narcotic it is readily dissipated by heat. If the leaves be chewed, the tongue will soon be covered with small ulcers. Taken internally, the juice has been known to cause death: it always has the effect of a violent purgative.

WOOD ANEMONE (*Anemone nemorosa*).—Cattle have been poisoned by eating Wood Anemone in a fresh state, but the plant in a dried state does not appear to be dangerous. The toxic principle is called *anemonin*, and is a very volatile body.

THE BUTTERCUP GROUP.—It is obviously necessary to examine this group with some care, as children love to gather buttercups, and sometimes play for hours with these flowers. Again, cattle must browse to an enormous extent on the commoner varieties, such as the Field Buttercup. It must, however, be pointed out that the whole of this group is pervaded by a deleterious substance, which varies in extent and degree according to the species and to the place where the plants are growing. In the Water Crowfoot the amount is so small as to be negligible, and the feeding properties which it otherwise possesses for cattle can be brought into play, for cows feed on it with avidity. The common buttercups, namely the Field Buttercup and the Bulbous Buttercup, have very acrid properties, the young fruits when green being the most dangerous. Taken internally the juice from the fruits has all the properties of a true acrid poison, and serious results have been known to ensue after eating the fruit of these Buttercups. The reason why horses and cattle have not been poisoned wholesale is due to the fact that they do not touch the Buttercups when in full leaf or flower, but only when dried in the form of hay; by this time the toxic substance has escaped, and the Buttercup has become a nutritious food. The *anemonin* stated above to be present in Anemone is also present in the Field and Bulbous Buttercups. A slice of the underground stem (corm) of the Bulbous Buttercup has been employed medicinally to cure toothache. The petals are dangerous when eaten in any quantity, but their acrid taste is fortunately a sufficient deterrent so far as children are concerned.

Fig. 25.—Lesser Spearwort (*Ranunculus Flammula*)

In Spearwort (fig. 25), which grows in wet places, the

toxic principle is present in greater quantity than in the plants mentioned above, and cattle browsing in boggy pastures, when this plant is present, run a very serious risk. More than one fatal case is on record in which horses and cattle have been killed through browsing on the Spearwort.

LESSER CELANDINE (*R. Ficaria*) has characteristic small club-shaped underground roots which, when young, are eaten as a salad; but a toxic substance is developed later, as the same roots when a little older are distinctly poisonous. They reach their most dangerous stage during the period of flowering.

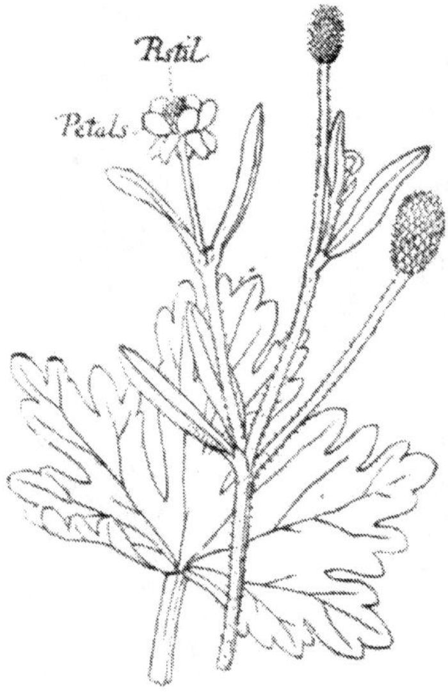

Fig. 26.—Celery-leaved Ranunculus (*Ranunculus Sceleratus*)

CELERY - LEAVED RANUNCULUS (*R. Sceleratus*) (fig. 26).—This plant is used by the tramp fraternity in the same way as Traveller's Joy. As in the case of other members of the orders, the poison is easily dissipated by heat. The chief danger from this herb arises from the resemblance its leaves bear to those of Parsley or Celery, and several cases are on record of disastrous results following the making of this mistake. Cattle have been known to die after eating this plant when they got it mixed up in their fodder.

MARSH MARIGOLD (*Caltha palustris*) (fig. 27).—In Germany the young buds are pickled like Capers. The same acrid poison which is common to the rest of the order is undoubtedly present in the Marsh Marigold, but it is not developed in the young plants. Cattle refuse to eat this plant when browsing in the open, but serious results have followed its careless introduction into their fodder.

Fig. 27.—Marsh Marigold (*Caltha palustris*)

THE HELLEBORES.—All three Hellebores are poisonous. They used to be much in favour with irregular practitioners, on account of the violent action of the juice of their members as purgatives. Unfortunately, other effects may also follow: in several cases the drinking of an infusion of Fetid Hellebore has been known to cause severe internal inflammation, with fatal results. It is easy to give an overdose, as in this family the poisonous

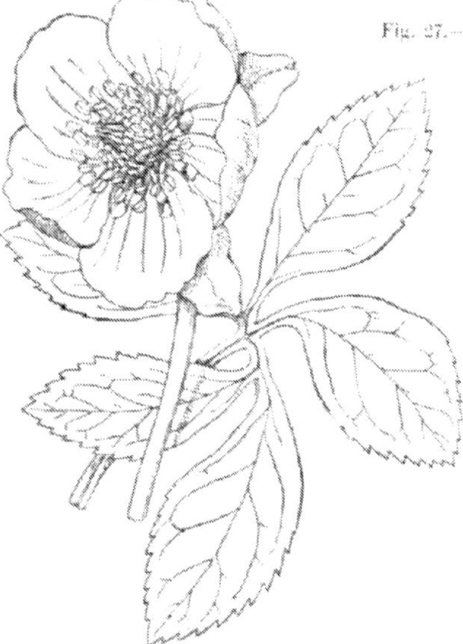

Fig. 28.—Black Hellebore (*Helleborus niger*)

preceded by convulsions. The strength of the poison can be estimated from the fact that $\frac{1}{16}$ of a grain of the alkaloid proved fatal in one case.

Fig. 29.—Aconite (*Aconitum Napellus*)

The greatest number of mishaps in connection with this plant have been due to its root being mistaken for that of horse-radish (see fig. 8). A comparison between these roots may not therefore be out of place:—

ACONITE.	HORSE-RADISH.
Tapering.	Cylindrical, not tapering.
Taste produces numbness of mouth and lips.	Hot and bitter to taste, but no numbness
White when cut, but slowly reddens.	White when cut; does not redden.
Secondary roots curly.	Secondary roots straight.

Monkshood should never be grown in a kitchen garden, as, though the roots of Monkshood and Horse-radish show marked difference when examined together, these are easily overlooked by the ignorant, who in most cases have never heard of Monkshood, and are not aware that any danger is to be feared from picking up its roots for those of Horse-radish.

Medicinal Properties.—When applied to the skin, preparations of Aconite produce a feeling of numbness. They are used extensively in certain forms of neuralgia and rheumatism. When taken internally, Aconite produces a steady fall of temperature and a lowering of the power to feel pain, so that it is given in cases of fever and pain.

Distribution.—Although not a native plant, Monkshood is very widely distributed in our gardens, and grows wild in some places in the West of England and South Wales.

Collection.—The root should be collected in autumn after the rest of the plant has died down.

Present Source of Supply.—Formerly the chief source was Switzerland. As this supply came via Germany it is probably cut off during the War. The price of the Continental root is 50*s.* a cwt. Japan is another source of supply, the root being derived from another species, *Aconitum Fischeri* This root commands about 35*s.* a cwt. The English root is ordinarily worth about 2*s.* a lb. The drug deteriorates rapidly in drying, and therefore a premium is set on the home-grown roots. Notwithstanding this, within recent years the cultivation of Aconite does not seem to have paid, though it is probable that as the price has practically doubled, its cultivation would, during the War at any rate, not be an unprofitable enterprise.

Cultivation.—The soil should be well dug, preferably shaded, and into it rotted leaves and stable manure should be pressed. Aconite can be raised from seed, but it takes two or three years to flower; it is therefore usually propagated from the smaller daughter-roots which form at the sides of the old roots. Replanting is usually done in December or January, the young roots being placed about a foot apart. Seeing that there are nearly sixty species of Monkshood, growers are careful to select the right kind, as the different species show great variation in their production of aconitine.

Fig. 30.—Columbine (*Aquilegia vulgaris*)

Columbine (*Aquilegia vulgaris*) (fig. 30).—The seeds are particularly harmful. Linnæus records that the seeds of Columbine proved fatal to some children who had eaten them.

Larkspur (*Delphinium*) (fig. 31).—The seeds are especially dangerous, and should be kept out of the way of children.

We may note with reference to the Ranunculaceæ that there is a kind of family resemblance in the poisons that are found in its various members. In general they are of the acrid, narcotic kinds; they lose their properties considerably when subjected to drying, because the poisons contained in them are of a volatile nature.

Papaveraceæ.—The members of this order are best recognized by the pistil (fig. 32). This is composed of many carpels joined together. When cut across, the compound ovary is seen to possess only one cavity, which, however, is divided up into a number of stalls, the number of stalls corresponding to the number of carpels that have made up the pistil. If the latter be examined once thoroughly, and bearing in mind that the type is peculiar to the Papaveraceæ, the reader should have little difficulty in recognizing the order in subsequent examinations. In

Fig. 31.—Larkspur (*Delphinium*)

Fig. 32.—*a*, Poppy Head (Pistil). *b*, Same, cut across.

addition, the order possesses the following characteristics:—

1. The petals are free.
2. The stamens are free and numerous.

Opium-Poppy (*Papaver somniferum*).—This is not a British plant, but is nevertheless a common object in our gardens, and could be more extensively and more profitably cultivated if desired. It is distinguished from the other members of the order by—

1. Its *smooth* stem and foliage.
2. Its flowers, which are white, but pinkish-purple at the base of the petals (fig. 33).

Opium is obtained by making horizontal incisions in the poppy-heads a few days after the fall of the flower. The milky juice which exudes in the form of tears is left on the plant for twenty-four hours, after which it is scraped off and made into cakes. This milky juice is also found in the petals; the seeds have very little of it, and, in fact, on account of the large amount of oil that they contain, they are eaten in some parts of Europe, being made into cakes. These cakes, when the oil has been expressed from them, also make excellent food for cattle.

Poisonous Properties.—Opium contains a large number of alkaloids, many being highly poisonous. The cases of poisoning which occur in this country are, however, confined exclusively to the abuse of various medicinal preparations. The symptoms of opium poisoning are drowsiness leading into insensibility, relaxation of muscles, clammy perspiration, and contraction of the pupils. The principal opium bases used in medicine are *morphine*, *codeine*, *apomorphine*, the first two being narcotics, the third an emetic.

There is no need to enter into a detailed description of the various officinal preparations—the patent medicines, soothing syrups, and various cordials which contain opium—the risk attendant on the abuse of such

Fig. 33. Opium Poppy (*Papaver somniferum*)

1, Capsule showing horizontal incisions. 2, Seed. 3, Section of seed.

fluids is well known. One drop of laudanum (tincture of opium) has on many occasions proved fatal to infants, the motive for its administration having been the ease of the mother rather than the well-being of the infant. Deaths from overdoses of opium are very common.

Medicinal Properties.—In experienced hands opium

is one of the most valuable of drugs, being administered to relieve pain and sooth excited nerves. It is also useful as an astringent in cases of diarrhœa, and as a sedative to ease coughs, &c.

Distribution.—The principal sources of opium are European and Asiatic Turkey, India, and China. In this country the white variety of Opium-Poppy is grown in several parts of the country, notably in Lincolnshire.

Collection.—In this country there is a steady market for poppy-heads, the capsules being harvested about September and placed for a fortnight on a drying floor. This is a boarded floor in a freely ventilated building; the capsules are placed in a thin layer on the floor, and are turned every day in order to secure uniformity of drying. The capsules are ready after they have become brittle, and crack in the hand when pressed.

Present Source of Supply.—In this country growers of Opium-Poppy supply the market only with poppy-heads. Belgium also, before the War, exported poppy-heads to this country. There is therefore a serious shortage, and Opium is one of the plants the cultivation of which is strongly recommended by the Board of Agriculture and Fisheries. Its cultivation would combine profit with patriotism, as there is likely to be a shortage for some years after the War. The price of the larger sizes is 12*s.* to 15*s.* per 1000, of the smaller sizes from 8*s.* to 10*s.* per 1000.

Cultivation.—Opium-Poppy grows best in a rich, moist soil, with plenty of sun. Usually it is cropped after wheat, oats, or barley. After manuring and ploughing in autumn, the seed is sown in March or April, 1 lb. of seed being allowed per acre. The drills are made a foot apart. When 3–4 inches high the plants are cut into clumps 6–9 inches apart, and then all except one are removed from the clump. If needed, a dressing of soot or some fertilizer is applied.

FIELD POPPY (*Papaver Rhœas*) (fig. 34).

1. Scarlet flowers.
2. Smooth round fruit.
3. Hairs on stalk of fruit of a spreading character.

Fig. 34.—Field Poppy (*Papaver Rhœas*)

The fresh petals are used in the making of a certain syrup; the flowers can only be utilized in this way if they are collected and packed off to their destination on the same day.

GREATER CELANDINE (*Chelidonium majus*) is easily recognized by its exudation, when bruised, of an orange-red juice. It has further a yellow flower, and a leaf of the shape shown in fig. 35.

This is an interesting herb, because it was a familiar medicinal plant of the Middle Ages, and its reputation as a healing agent was the cause of its introduction into this country, for it is not strictly a native plant. The old name was SWALLOW-WORT. The acrid juice is still an old country remedy for the curing of warts. Internally it acts as a purgative, but one that is not without risk, as a juice which can produce an effect on warts is apt to be drastic when applied to the sensitive lining of the stomach and intestines. If the tip of the tongue be applied to the orange-red juice, some idea of its acrid and nauseous character will be obtained. Five alkaloids, two acids, and a neutral bitter principle have been extracted from the exuding juice.

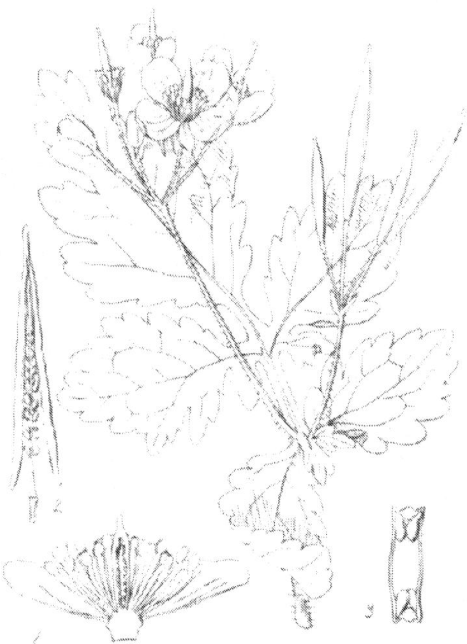

Fig. 35.—Greater Celandine (*Chelidonium majus*)

1, Section of flower. 2, Fruit. 3, Cross-section of fruit.

Mr. Holmes places the Greater Celandine in a list of plants that are required by the hundredweight.

Violaceæ.—There is no need to describe in detail the characteristics of this order, as its members are confined to the Violets and Pansies, which are known to all.

Sweet Violet (*Viola odorata*).—This sweet-smelling

herb was supposed, in the Middle Ages, to be capable of curing many diseases. Its downfall is great, for at present its only medicinal use is that of a slight laxative, usually prescribed to young children. The juice from the roots excites nausea, vomiting, and "nerves". The seeds of the Sweet Violet are sometimes prescribed as a purgative.

Fig. 36.—Arrangement of Stamens in Cruciferæ

Among the many "cures" for cancer, one is an infusion of the fresh leaves of the Sweet Violet. The flowers figure in the list of plants imported into this country from the Continent; they are used in making *syrup of violets*. The flowers are cut just before they begin to expand, and dried on trays in a warm, well-ventilated room.

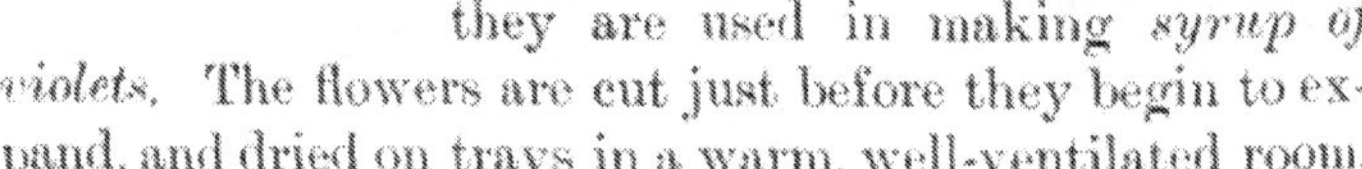

THE CRUCIFERÆ

A very important Natural Order, and one which includes many esculents and few poisonous or medicinal plants. The distinctive marks are the following:—

1. *Petals*, four in number, and usually arranged crosswise.
2. Six *stamens*, two of which are arranged *outside* the other four. Usually the inner four are longer than the two outside stamens (fig. 36).
3. A very characteristic *fruit*, and one peculiar to the Cruciferæ. The seeds are liberated by a split which begins at the bottom and gradually extends to the top (fig. 37).

Fig. 37.—Fruit of Cruciferæ (siliqua)

The most characteristic feature for purposes of identification is the second of the above, for while many orders have flowers with six stamens, not one other has these arranged in the manner they are in the Cruciferæ.

HORSE-RADISH (*Cochlearia Armoracia*).—A volatile oil, called *allyl isothiocyanate*, is present in the root of Horse-radish, which gives to it its pleasant pungency. The oil is used in medicine as a stimulant. Its chief use, however, is as a condiment, although the plant figures in a list of plants required by herbalists.

SCURVY GRASS (*Cochlearia officinalis*).—This herb is easily distinguished from others of the same order by—

1. Its spoon-shaped leaves.
2. Its small, *globular*, fleshy fruits (about 2 millimetres diameter).

It stands about a foot from the ground; where growing on stony ground it is much smaller.

When eaten fresh the plant is a refreshing stimulant; but formerly, as suggested by its name, far-reaching healing virtues were attributed to it.

THE MUSTARDS.—These are by far the most important medicinal plants among the Cruciferæ. There are three Mustards of importance:—

	PODS.	LEAF.
WHITE MUSTARD (fig. 38).	Bristly.	Deeply cut into segments from the edge almost to the mid-rib.
BLACK MUSTARD (fig. 39).	Smooth, four-sided.	Lower leaves pinnate, upper ones narrow, pointed, undivided.
WILD MUSTARD (CHARLOCK)(fig 40).	Rugged, with many angles.	Rough and toothed.

As a further help, it is useful to remember that the Black Mustard is taller than the other two, but its flowers have smaller petals Charlock has characteristic spreading sepals, and is very abundant in cornfields. Another useful point to remember is that the seeds of the White Mustard are 2 millimetres, and those of the Black Mustard 1 millimetre in diameter.

The powdered seeds are used for making poultices. "Mustard leaves" consist of paper to the surface of which the crushed seeds (deprived of fixed oil) have been made to adhere.

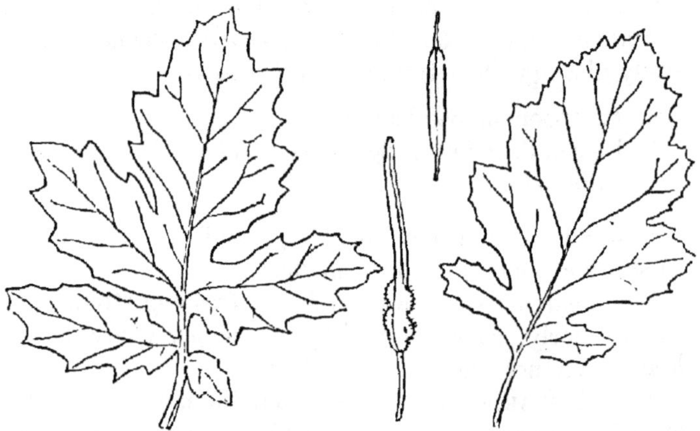

Fig. 38 —White Mustard Fig 39 —Black Mustard

The innocence or guilt of the Charlock in producing injurious effects is an important matter, owing to its abundance in cornfields, and the consequent risk of its appearing later in flour and ultimately in our bread. A really poisonous Crucifer is, however, unknown, and Charlock, notwithstanding Linnæus' comment on it, is quite an innocent plant.

Although Mustard was cultivated in this country before the War, most of our supplies came from the Continent, indicating that we had not attended sufficiently to the cultivation of an essentially native, medicinal plant.

As a family the members of the Cruciferæ neither

mend nor mar the body. Mishaps have occurred through eating Crucifers, e.g. Watercress, but in such cases the evil resides not in the plant itself, but in something that

Fig. 40.—Wild Mustard (Charlock)

1. Flower (petals removed). 2. Petal. 3. Fruit.

has entered it from the outside and which is not a normal constituent. In the case of Watercress the bacilli of typhoid fever are apt to gain entrance into the plant if the latter is growing in sewage-contaminated water.

Caryophyllaceæ.—Campion and Stitchwort Family.
Distinguishing characteristics:—

1. Free petals.
2. Opposite leaves.
3. Stem swollen at the joints.

Soapwort (*Saponaria officinalis*).—A robust plant, about 2-4 feet high, with broad, pointed leaves. The pink flowers are arranged in a bunch at the top in such a way that they all stand at the same level (corymb). It became naturalized in Britain in the Middle Ages, being then used as a drug. The root has a sharp burning taste, induces sneezing, and is poisonous. When mixed with water it readily forms a lather, this being due to the presence in it, to the extent of about 34 per cent, of a substance called *saponin*, which readily forms a froth when mixed with water.

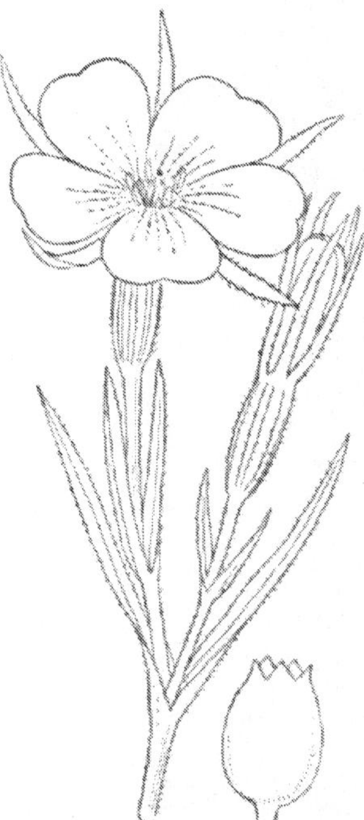

Fig. 41.—Corn Cockle (*Agrostemma Githago*)

Corn Cockle (*Agrostemma Githago*) (fig. 41).—This poisonous plant is distinguished from the other members of the order by its large handsome purple-red flowers, which appear in June or July. Accidents from eating the seeds of Corn Cockle are confined to cattle, the seeds being sometimes found in large quantities in the fodder of these animals. It has been stated that 2½ parts of these seeds in 1000 parts of fodder will kill a fowl. The adulteration can be readily detected by observing through a microscope the structure of the starch grains inside the seed. These grains are peculiar in shape, and quite different from the starch grains found in cereals. Accidents to human beings are unknown, because the poison in Corn Cockle seeds is destroyed during the process of baking.

LESSER STITCHWORT (*Stellaria graminea*).—On the Continent there have been numerous complaints of poisonous effects, from this very common hedge-plant, to horses and cattle. It can be identified by its *deeply-cut white petals* and erect, angular, and smooth stalk.

CHAPTER VI

POLYPETALÆ (*Continued*)

Leguminosæ.—Pea and Bean Family. This is an extremely important family, as from its members are obtained nutritious foods, valuable medicines, and virulent poisons. The characteristics of the family are easily recognized. The flowers of Gorse, Broom, and Laburnum obviously belong to the same Natural Order; in fact, the flowers of this order present so marked a difference from practically all other flowers that they can be identified without submitting them to a detailed examination of the various parts.

The flower has 5 petals, two joined to form a partially enclosed box called the "keel", two arranged laterally and called *wings*, and one large erect petal called the *standard*. There are 10 stamens—in some flowers all, in others only nine, being arranged in a circle, their stalks united to form a hollow tube (fig. 42). Inside this staminal tube is situated the pistil, which in this case is made up of only one carpel. Lastly, the fruit is characteristic, being a pod showing one cavity inside of which is a single row of seeds. A Pea-pod is a familiar example. All the other species have similar fruits, though naturally there are differences in size, colour, texture, &c.

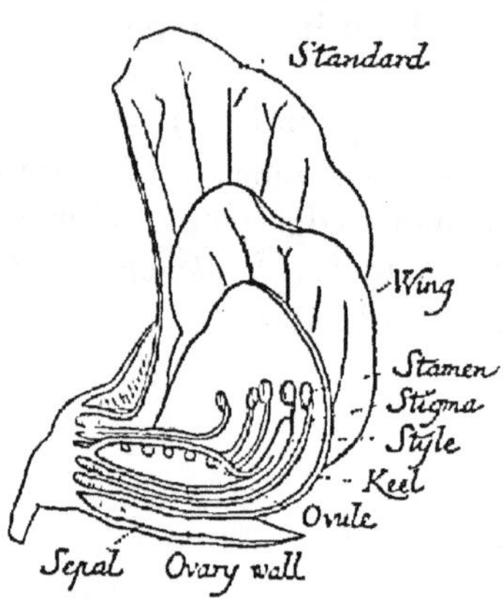

Fig 42.—Section of Leguminous Flower

LABURNUM (see Chapter X).

BROOM (*Cytisus scoparius*).—Superficially it is not easy to distinguish the Broom from the Laburnum when the latter is a small shrub, but the Broom has *stiff green branches* and *small leaves*, both features being sufficiently uncommon to permit of the immediate identification of the plant.

Poisonous Properties.—When Broom tops are eaten by sheep they produce excitation and, later, stupefaction. This is caused by a very poisonous and narcotic principle in the tops called *sparteine*, and to another poisonous substance called *scoparin*.

Medicinal Properties.—These poisonous principles are very valuable medicinally because they increase the action of the bowels and of the kidneys, and are of great use in certain complaints.

Distribution.—Found wild in open country, particularly in gravelly soils.

Collection.—Young shoots are cut in May.

LUPIN (*Lupinus*).—This garden plant is recognized by

its spike of blue[1] flowers and its digitate leaves, these being spread out like the fingers on the hand.

One species (*Lupinus albus*) was cultivated by the ancients on account of the food value of its seeds, and in France this species is cultivated to-day in order to supply food for sheep. Some species of Lupin are, however, indubitably poisonous, and therefore experiments on this species with the view of increasing our supply of food or fodder should only be undertaken by experts.

SCARLET RUNNER (*Phaseolus multiflorus*).—The root is poisonous.

YELLOW VETCHLING (*Lathyrus Aphaca*).—The seeds have been known to cause headache and vomiting.

MELILOT (*Melilotus officinalis*).—From this plant was prepared an old-fashioned but now almost obsolete remedy for rheumatism.

In the lists of plants used by herbalists only three of the Leguminosæ appear, viz. Broom, Melilot, and Fenugreek. With regard to the last-named, Mr. Holmes states that it is doubtful whether it would pay to cultivate it in this country, though it grows readily here. Its habitat is West Asia.

Rosaceæ.—This important order contains the vast majority of our fruits, such as Apple, Pear, Strawberry, Cherry, &c. As is shown below, it contains within its fold also a few medicinal, as well as a few poisonous plants. The recognition of members of this order is not always easy. All the flowers have free petals, numerous stamens, just as the Ranunculaceæ have, but in the Rosaceæ the perigynous condition always holds (see fig. 7 for explanation). Sometimes the perigyny is difficult to distinguish from hypogyny. For example, the Water Avens (Rosaceæ) would by most beginners be placed among the Ranunculaceæ. It is a good rule

[1] Sometimes white, yellow, or lilac.

to remember that in *all* perigynous flowers the stamens are *not in contact with the ovary*. This is shown in fig. 7. In hypogynous flowers the stamens arise from just underneath the ovary, whilst in the epigynous flowers the stamens arise from the upper part of the ovary. A flower, therefore, which shows perigyny in addition to the possession of free petals and numerous stamens can be safely regarded as a member of the Rosaceæ. The main divisions of this important family are the following:—

I. **The Almond Group (Amygdaleæ).**—

Characteristics:—

Pistil = 1 carpel (fig. 5, *b*).

Fruit, a *drupe*—that is, the single seed is enclosed by two envelopes, the inner hard, the outer soft.

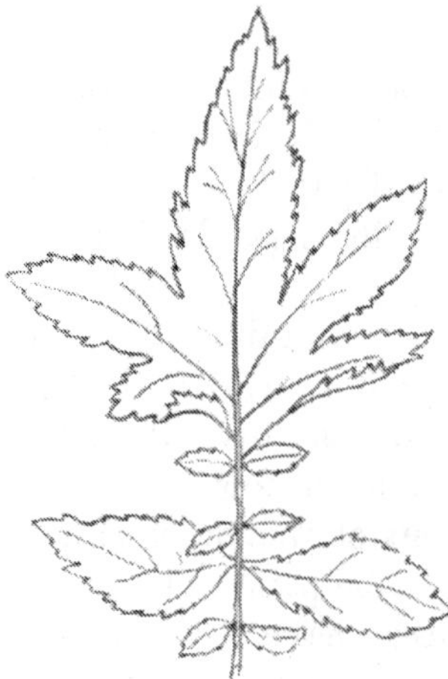

Fig. 43.—Pinnate Leaves of Meadow-sweet

All are shrubs or trees, and will therefore receive treatment in Chapter X.

II. **Meadow-sweet Group (Spireidæ).**—In the leaflet issued by the Board of Agriculture and Fisheries it is stated that a larger quantity than usual of the *Meadow-sweet* (*Spiræa Ulmaria*) will need to be gathered next season. The leaves are *pinnate* (i.e. paired), the alternate pairs being smaller (fig. 43); the flowers are *yellowish-white* and very fragrant. The herb is very common on moist meadows. The flowers yield a fragrant distilled water, whilst the roots are astringent.

III. **The Strawberry Group (Potentilleidæ).**—The flower of this group resembles the Buttercup in its general build, but differs in that it is *perigynous*. If the stamens be pulled aside, it will be found that they are not placed close up against the carpels, but form a ring a little apart from them (fig. 7*b*). In all the members the *calyx is persistent*, a fact which furnishes a very useful feature for diagnostic purposes. The fruits of the Strawberry, Bramble, and Raspberry are succulent; the rest, however, form a dry fruit. The carpels are many (fig. 7*b*).

COMMON AGRIMONY (*Agrimonia Eupatoria*).—*Characteristics:*—

1. Yellow flower.
2. Pinnate leaves, each alternate pair being smaller.

These characteristics, in addition to those common to the whole group, serve to identify this plant with ease. The herb is aromatic and tonic, and is in demand by herbalists. It is commonly made into tea. The whole herb is picked in July.

THE WOOD AVENS (*Geum urbanum*).—The leaves of this herb are shown in fig. 44. The flowers are erect and yellow. The fruits have *long-pointed awns hooked at the end*. It is quite a common plant, and flowers from June to August. In olden days it was much used in culinary operations on account of its aromatic odour. Incidentally it was also used in the travails of the soul for warding off evil spirits. The root is astringent, owing to the presence of tannic acid. It has also

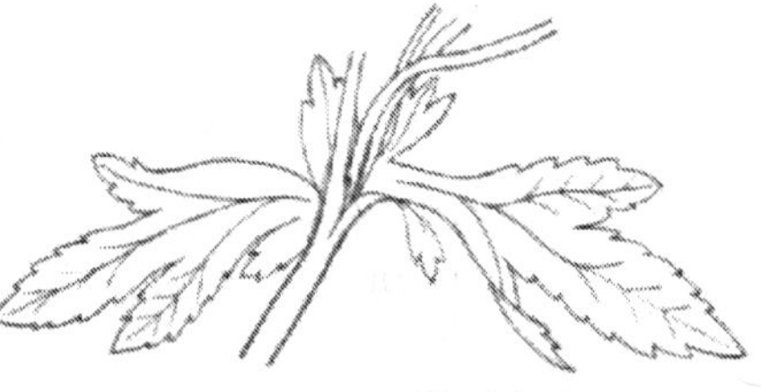

Fig. 44.—Leaves of Wood Avens

a little volatile oil, gum, a bitter substance called geum-bitter, and small quantities of other substances. The *Radix Caryophyllatæ* of the pharmacists is the dried root and underground stem of this plant. The Avens is also in demand by the herbalists.

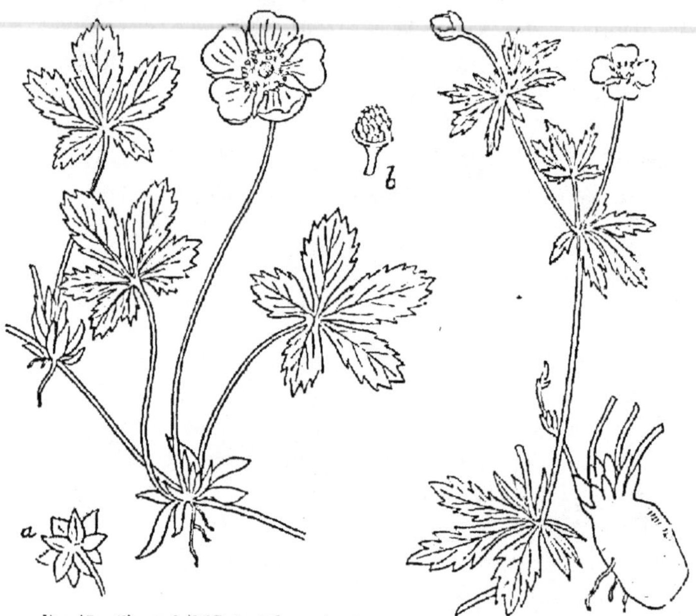

Fig. 45.—Cinquefoil (*Potentilla reptans*)
a, Calyx seen from below. *b*, Head of achenes

Fig. 46.—Tormentil (*Potentilla Tormentilla*)

WATER AVENS (*Geum rivale*).—The aromatic, astringent, and antiseptic root of this herb was used in the Middle Ages in making beer, just as hops are used at the present day. In the United States it is used as a tonic and as a febrifuge. It is distinguished from the preceding herb by the possession of large reddish-purple flowers, and the whole plant is hairy.

The TORMENTIL (*Potentilla Tormentilla*) and the CINQUEFOIL (*Potentilla reptans*).—Both of these are yellow-flowered plants, and very common in open, moorland country. The Tormentil has a cross-shaped flower, about ⅓ inch (fig. 46); the flower of Cinquefoil is larger, has 5 petals, and its leaves are of the palmate type (fig. 45). In the past the Cinquefoil was credited with being a curative agent for cancer, jaundice, gout, and other ailments. Its reputation, however, has long since been shattered. The roots of Tormentil are in demand by herbalists on account of their tonic and astringent qualities; they further contain from 18 to 30 per cent of *tannic acid.*

IV. **The Burnet Group (Sanguisorbidæ).**—This group is not important for our purpose, although its members have astringent or tonic properties.

V. **The Rose Group (Rosidæ).**

THE RED OR PROVENCE ROSE (*Rosa gallica*).—The petals of the scented red roses of the *Rosa gallica* and *Rosa damascena* group are imported into this country, being used medicinally or for *pot-pourri.*

Medicinal Properties.—From the petals a pleasant astringent infusion is made.

Collection.—The whole of the petals are removed just before they expand.

Present Source of Supply.—Several British growers have lately given up growing this plant for medicinal purposes on account of various difficulties; and as the Continental supply is at present cut off, there will be a scarcity for some time. The petals usually realize 3s. to 4s. per lb. when dry, but will of course now be more valuable.

VI. **The Apple Group (Pomeæ).**—There are no medicinal or poisonous plants in this section, although it should be noted that the leaves of the *Mountain Ash* (*Pyrus Aucuparia*) yield a trace of prussic acid on analysis, and that the seeds of the whole group must be regarded with suspicion. The commoner members are Apple, Pear, Mountain Ash, Hawthorn, Medlar, and Cotoneaster.

The Umbelliferæ or Hemlock Family.—A very important group, and fortunately one that is easily identified if a little care be taken. As the name implies, the flowers are placed at the end of the rays of an *umbel*; that is to say, the stalks bearing the flowers are arranged as are the rays of an umbrella, radiating from one point (fig. 47). Usually each stalk of the umbel itself bears a little secondary umbel (fig. 47), and each stalk of the secondary umbel carries a small flower at the end of it. For the identification of the order, the following points will be sufficient:—

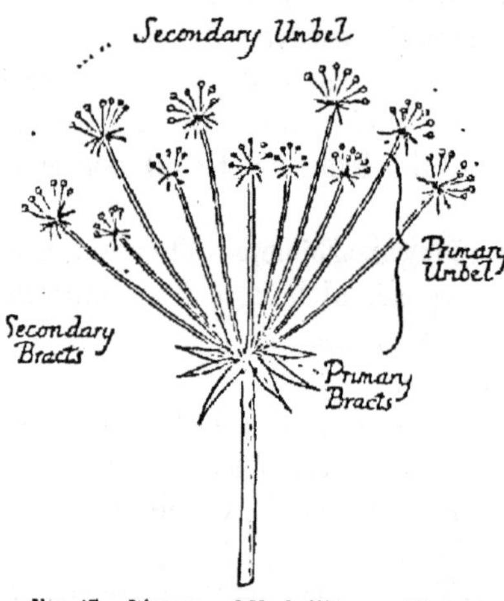

Fig. 47.—Diagram of Umbelliferous Flower

1. Flowers arranged in umbels.
2. Flowers white.
3. Flowers with inferior ovary.

All three points can easily be noted, but in some cases it is not so easy to distinguish the individual species from one another, because, superficially at any rate, a large number of the species are very much alike. It is necessary to distinguish the species with accuracy, for the reason that the order includes medicinal and kitchen herbs as well as dangerous and poisonous plants. The organ which shows the greatest amount of variation in form is the *fruit*, to which close attention should be paid in the examination of any particular species. This variation may be seen by a comparison of figs. 48–51, 54–59. Another great aid to identification is this, that while in some members of the order there are small leaves (bracts) at the base of both primary and secondary umbels (see fig. 47), in others the bracts are confined to the primary or to the secondary umbels, in still others they are absent from both umbels. A knowledge of these differences considerably facilitates identification in the field of the various Umbellifers. The two carpels of which the pistil is composed separate on fruiting, each being held to the stalk by a thin thread called the carpophore (see fig. 48). In the same figure are shown the canals filled with oil (called vittæ), which are situated between the ribs (fig. 48).

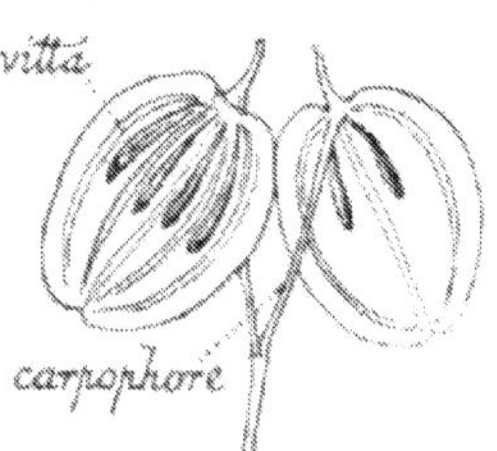

Fig. 48.—Fruit of Umbelliferæ

Poison Hemlock (*Conium maculatum*).—This is perhaps the Umbellifer around which the most interest centres. A knowledge of its properties dates from very early times. Hemlock juice probably formed the fatal draught Socrates was compelled to drink, after he had been indicted for "reviling the gods acknowledged by the State". Apart from the umbrella-like appearance which distinguishes all the members of the Umbelliferæ, Hemlock is distinguished specifically by the following characteristics:—

1. The stem is hollow, and *marked with spots of a dull-red colour*.
2. The shape of the fruit (see fig. 49, *a* and *b*).
3. The glossy dark-green shining appearance of the

leaves, and, when bruised, their "dead-mouse" odour.

Poisonous Properties.—Cases of poisoning from eating this plant are of common occurrence. In one case some boys from an Industrial school partook of Hemlock whilst picnicking on the island of Cumbrae (Firth of Clyde), mistaking the root for an edible herb. Almost at once twenty-four of the boys were taken ill; in this case all except one recovered. Recently a case of fatal poisoning was reported from the Isle of Man. The symptoms of poisoning from Hemlock are deep stupor and loss of the use of the limbs.

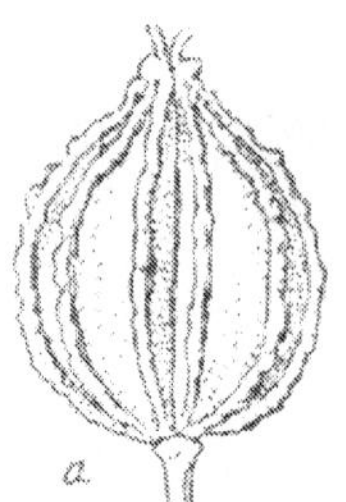

Fig. 49.—*a*, Fruit of Hemlock. *b*, Section of same.

Of the substances extracted from the plant the chief is *coniine* (½–1 per cent). This is a colourless oily liquid with an unpleasant mouse-like odour and a biting taste. Others are *methyl-coniine*, *conhydrine*, and *ethyl-piperidine*. It is interesting to note that these substances are volatile, and therefore it is not difficult to extract the poisonous principles; in fact, it is stated that formerly Hemlock leaves (thoroughly cooked) were eaten as a vegetable. Larks and quails eat the Hemlock without suffering any ill effects, but their flesh afterwards is dangerous for human beings to eat.

Medicinal Properties.—The juice prepared from the Hemlock is used as a sedative and narcotic in various spasmodic diseases.

Distribution.—Hemlock is generally distributed over the whole of Great Britain; it grows better in shady places.

Collection.—The herb and unripe fruits are collected in June from second-year plants. Hemlock is a biennial.

Present Source of Supply.—Both the herb and fruit are in request by the wholesale druggist and herbalist. We appear to use about half a ton in the year. Since the outbreak of the War the price has nearly doubled.

Water Hemlock or Cowbane (*Cicuta virosa*).—A deadly poisonous plant. Superficially it is not unlike Hemlock. To distinguish them the following points must be noted:—

1. The shape of the leaves (see fig. 50) Note that the segments of these are *long*, *narrow*, and *serrated*.
2. There are no bracts on the main umbel, but these are present on the secondary umbel.
3. The root is white, fleshy, and contains a *yellow* juice.

The resemblance of the root to celery or parsnip is the chief source of danger. In this organ the *coniine* contained in Hemlock is also present in Cowbane, as well as another poisonous substance, *cicutoxin*, which has a disagreeable acid taste. The presence of this latter poison is a fortunate circumstance, as its acrid property prevents the plant being eaten in large quantities. In spite of this, however, fatal cases of poisoning have been recorded.

Hemlock Water Dropwort (*Œnanthe crocata*).—This is a tall plant which grows commonly in ditches, and can be recognized by the following characteristics:—

1. The stem is hollow and channelled.
2. The fruit is egg-shaped, with ridges that are not prominent.

3. The roots exude a white juice when bruised, which becomes yellow on drying.
4. Each plant has five or more spindle-shaped roots in attachment.

Fig. 50.—Water Hemlock or Cowbane (*Cicuta virosa*)

a, Flower. *b*, Fruit. *c*, Cross-section of fruit. *d*, Root.

A comparison with fig. 51 will make these points clear.

The root is the most deadly part of the plant, on account of its resemblance to parsnips. According to Henslow, cattle have been poisoned by eating the roots, thrown upon the land, when the ditches have been cleared. The danger is rendered more acute by the fact that the poisons contained in the root are not destroyed

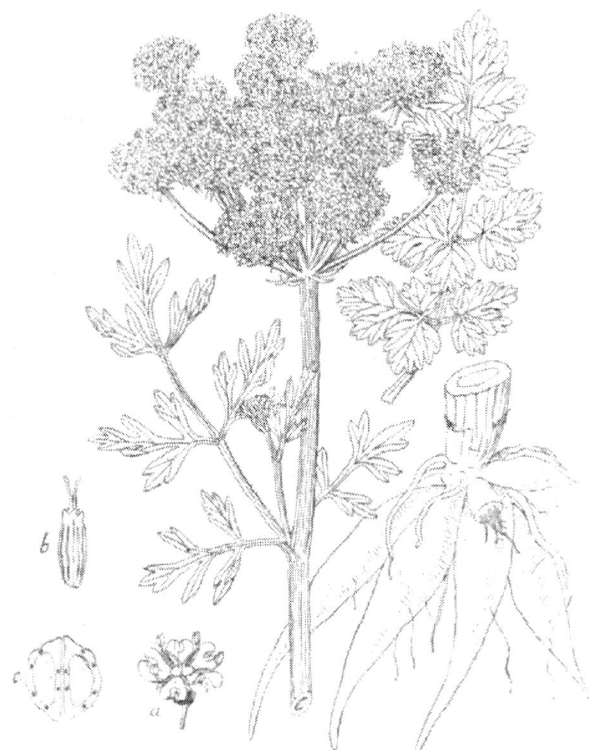

Fig. 51.—Hemlock Water Dropwort (*Œnanthe crocata*)

a, Flower. *b*, Fruit. *c*, Cross-section of fruit.

by drying or cooking. As an example of the effects of poisoning from this plant, we may take the following: One man took two bites of the root and then threw it away. The first symptom produced was vomiting; this was followed by a state of drowsiness but not of insensibility; his face became pale, and he showed dilated pupils. Finally, after treatment he recovered.

COMMON WATER DROPWORT (*Œnanthe fistulosa*).—This is also a poisonous herb, but considerably less so than the preceding. Although somewhat similar in general habit the leaves are different, being composed only of a few narrow segments (fig. 52). The roots also are different, consisting of clustered fibres or of oblong tuberous structures. Finally, the sepals of the flowers are unusually large. Animals refuse to eat the plant.

Fig. 52.—Common Water Dropwort (*Œnanthe fistulosa*)

a, Cluster of florets. *b*, Single floret

COW PARSNIP OF HOGWEED (*Heracleum Sphondylium*).—This coarse-looking plant is very familiar on waste grounds and in hedges It can be recognized at once from the leaf, which is large, broad, and rough; it is also pinnate, and all the pinnæ are stalkless except the basal pair (fig. 53) Again, the fruit has a distinctive disk-like shape (fig. 48). The smell of this coarse plant is sufficient to prevent its being eaten, but a case is reported from Belgium of workmen having been affected after *collecting* the plant. They had been employed to root it out from a certain park. This was done in the early morning at a season of great heat. All experienced intense heat on the left arm and wrist. Inflammation followed, accompanied by sores which prevented them from returning to work

Fig. 53.—Cow Parsnip or Hogweed (*Heracleum Sphondylium*)

a, Flower. *b*, Fruit. *c*, Fruit cut across

for nearly three weeks. In collecting the plants they had thrown them over their left arm, with the result that the volatile oil, which during the later parts of the day would have volatilized, had condensed on their arms and produced the effects stated.

A few of the other Umbellifers are not above suspicion of possessing poisonous qualities. It is strange that one of these should be the WILD CARROT (*Daucus Carota*), the root of the cultivated variety of this species being so widely used as a vegetable; but the fact remains that white mice have been killed through being given the root of the Wild Carrot to eat. The active principle in this root is a volatile oil called *pinene*. The Wild Carrot may be recognized by the prominent ridges of the fruit (fig. 54) and the peculiar structure of the bracts. Others of the same nature are the WATER PARSNIP (*Sium latifolium*) and BEAKED PARSLEY (*Anthriscus sylvestris*), although these seem to have very little effect on cattle and other animals.

Fig. 54.—Wild Carrot (*Daucus Carota*)

a, Flower. *b*, Fruit. *c*, Fruit (larger scale) cut across.

The medicinal plants in the Umbelliferæ are numerous, and form an important percentage of the plants collected by the druggist and herbalist.

DILL (*Peucedanum graveolens*).—There are three species of Peucedanum native to this country, but Dill is not one of them, being a native of Southern Europe. It may be included, however, for the following reasons, viz., that it can be and is cultivated in England, that we use medicinally between two and three tons of the drug annually, and that it was imported largely from Germany before the War.

It may be recognized by—

1. The shape of the leaves.
2. The flat shape of the fruit. (See fig. 55.)

Medicinal Properties.—Dill is much used as an aromatic stimulant and carminative. The fruit contains 3 to 4 per cent of *volatile oil.* The aroma s due to a substance called *carvol* which s present in the oil. The leaves, gathered n July and August, re used for pickling, nd also for flavourng soups.

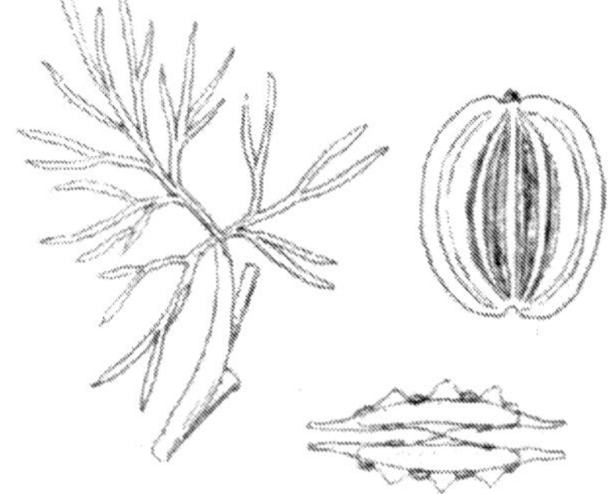

Fig. 55.—Dill (*Peucedanum graveolens*)

Cultivation.—It is ecommended to sow ie seeds in September, or at any time between February id May, in drills 1 inch apart; the seedlings should e thinned till they are 10 inches apart. Any friable irden soil in an open situation is suitable. 10 lb. of ed should be drilled to the acre, which should yield cwt. of the fruit.

British-grown Dill fetches a better price than the reign variety because of its cleaner appearance and eedom from weed seeds. Dill seems to grow very well the heavy soil of Essex.

Garden Angelica (*Angelica Archangelica*).—This is tall, coarse-growing herb, the leaf-stalks of which at e time were bleached and eaten like celery, or candied d used as a confection. It is easily propagated by seeds. In addition, the fruit contains a volatile oil and other constituents, so that the plant is in request as an aromatic stimulant. It can be most easily identified by the fruit, which has five wing-like ridges and a pleasantly aromatic odour and taste. It is not a British plant, and must not be confused with the WILD ANGELICA (*A. sylvestris*), which is a white-flowered Umbellifer with leaves of the shape shown in fig. 56. The writer has heard it stated that the Garden Angelica was first brought to this country, and used as a seasoning and in confectionery, by Mary Queen of Scots, who is said to have brought it from France.

Fig. 56.—Wild Angelica (*A. sylvestris*)
a, Flower. *b*, Section of fruit. *c*, Fruit

The Fennel Group.

COMMON FENNEL (*Fœniculum vulgare*).—This herb is easily recognized by its leaves, which consist of a number of deeply-divided, hair-like segments (fig. 57), and large terminal umbels of *yellow* flowers. The whole plant is aromatic, and its chopped leaves are often used as an ingredient in sauce for fish. It grows in waste places, especially near the sea. For the propagation of Common Fennel, seeds are sown in drills in the autumn.

The Fennel of the druggists consists of the dried ripe fruit of *Fœniculum capillaceum.* It is a native of

Southern Europe, but is cultivated in this country. It grows best on stiff soils in sunny situations. The seeds are sown in spring, 5 lb. being allowed to the acre, the

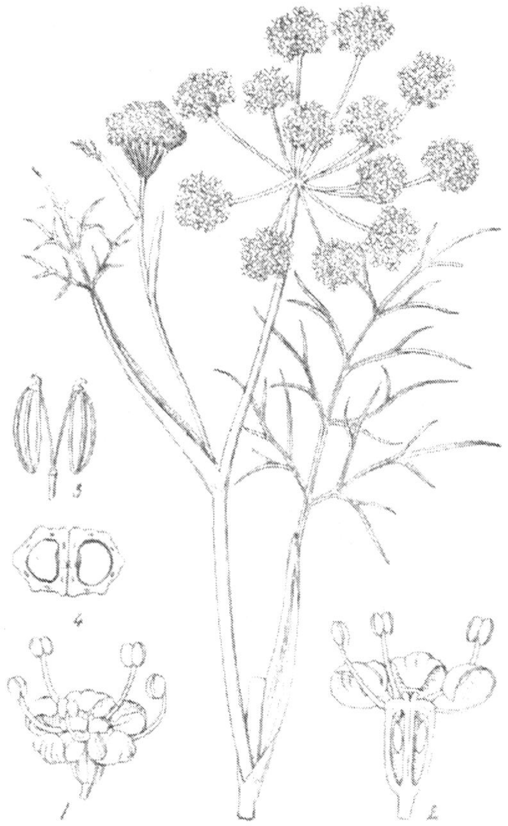

Fig. 57.—Common Fennel (*Fœniculum vulgare*)

1, Flower. 2, Flower section. 3, Fruit. 4, Section of fruit.

ield therefrom being about 15 cwt. It sells at from l to £1, 5*s.* per cwt. Fennel varies much in sweetness d flavour, and the British varieties are not the best in e market. Mr. Holmes recommends the cultivation of a good strain of Fennel in this country. Seeing that so much difference in sweetness and flavour prevails among the different varieties of this herb, it is very probable that these are properties which would lend themselves to improvement by careful cultivation.

The fruit has five ridges, the lateral ones being broader than the others. From it is extracted a light-yellow volatile oil, which is employed as an aromatic stimulant and as a cure for flatulency.

THE ANISE FAMILY (*Pimpinella*).—The two British representatives of *Pimpinella* are the BURNET SAXIFRAGE (*Pimpinella Saxifraga*) and *Pimpinella magna*. The roots of the former are used by herbalists, but it is not a plant of any importance. The Aniseed of the pharmacist is a native of Southern and Central Europe. It is, however, grown for commercial purposes in North Germany, and the writer has seen it growing in Scotland. The leaves are valuable adjuncts for seasoning certain dishes, and medicinally the fruit is in great request on account of its sweet aromatic taste and smell, due to the presence in it of 2 to 3 per cent of a volatile oil. As we use as much as 100 tons of this plant annually, the possibility of its successful cultivation for commercial purposes should be seriously considered. *Pimpinella Anisum*, as this species is named, is most easily identified by examining the fruit, which, unlike all other Umbelliferous fruits, is compressed laterally, and presents a rough appearance from the presence of short bristly hairs (fig. 58). It is about $\frac{1}{8}$ inch long and $\frac{1}{12}$ inch broad.

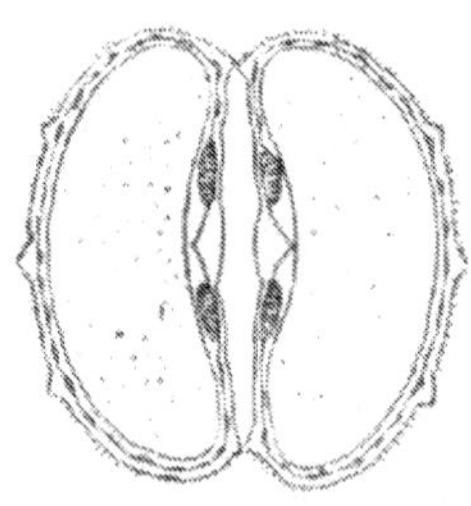

Fig. 58.—Fruit of *Pimpinella Anisum*, enlarged

Propagation is effected by seeds, which are sown in

April on a southern exposure in lines 1 foot apart. The seedlings are afterwards thinned to 6 inches in the line. Aniseed grows best in a light and sandy soil.

The COMMON CARAWAY (*Carum Carvi*) is the most important of this family. It can be recognized by the following characteristics:—

1. A spindle-shaped root.
2. A much-branched stem 2 feet high.
3. Twice-pinnate leaves, with leaflets cut into very narrow segments.
4. White flowers, *with only one bract at the base of the general umbel.*
5. Fruits *tapering at each end*, and possessing an agreeable aromatic odour and spicy taste.

The fruit contains from $3\frac{1}{2}$ to $6\frac{1}{2}$ per cent of volatile oil, which is valuable as a stimulant and is used for curing flatulency. The residue, after the removal of the oil, forms a valuable food for cattle owing to its proteins and fats. The seeds have long been valued by confectioners and cooks.

This plant was formerly extensively cultivated in Essex and Kent, but of late years its cultivation in this country seems to have been discontinued. Possibly the new conditions brought about by the War may revive its cultivation. Before 1914 it was imported from Morocco, Holland, Russia, and Germany.

British Caraway fetches a better price in the market, because of its freedom from other seeds and cleaner appearance. The Common Caraway must not be confused with the two native Caraway plants, which are not used medicinally; these are the WHORLED CARAWAY (*C. verticillatum*) and the BULBOUS CARAWAY (*C. Bulbocastanum*).

COMMON CORIANDER (*Coriandrum sativum*).—This plant, although not a native, is found occasionally in the neighbourhood of towns. As the fruit contains a valuable volatile oil, the plant is extensively cultivated. It is a hardy annual, growing about 2 feet high, and bearing white flowers in June or later, according to the time of sowing. The fruit is shown in section in fig. 59. It has an agreeable aromatic odour, especially when bruised, and also an agreeable taste. The volatile oil which it contains is made up to the extent of 90 per cent of *coriandrol*, which is valuable as a stimulant and has aromatic and stomachic properties. The leaves are also in demand for flavouring soups and for dressing salads.

Fig 59.—Section of Fruit of Coriander

For the cultivation of Coriander, seeds are sown in warm positions in spring and autumn. It grows on ordinary soils. Before the War Coriander was imported from Bombay, Morocco, Russia, and Germany. Its price to-day is more than double what it was in 1914, when it fetched from 16s. to 30s. a cwt.

CELERY (*Apium graveolens*).—It is worth noting that the dried fruit of the Celery produces a volatile oil which is used medicinally as a stimulant and for curing flatulency. The Celery of the gardens has been derived by careful cultivation and selection from the British wild Celery. The latter, however, is suspect, its root, although in shape and odour resembling that of the cultivated Celery, is very acrid and not fit for eating.

Review of the Umbelliferæ.—The Umbellifers of this country that are either poisonous or medicinal fall readily into two classes—the Aromatic series, including Celery, Coriander, Caraway, Anise, Fennel, and Dill; and the non-aromatic poisonous Cow Parsnip, Water Dropwort, Water Hemlock, and Hemlock. The following outstanding features will help the reader to identify the more important: An aromatic Umbellifer with *yellow* flowers indicates *Fennel*, one with white flowers and aromatic *globular* fruit is probably *Coriander*. *Anise* is peculiar in possessing a fruit clothed with short bristly hairs. The structure of the leaves of Dill is very unlike that of most Umbellifers. Again, the fact that the main umbel of Caraway possesses *only one bract* constitutes a very distinctive feature. With regard to Celery, the characteristic odour and flavour which we associate with this plant is perhaps its best beacon.

The identification of the non-aromatic Umbellifers must be carried out in the same way, i.e. by picking out individual characteristics after having first ascertained that the plant in question is an Umbellifer. Thus, *Hemlock* has its odour and its red spots, *Water Dropwort* and *Water Hemlock* have their yellow exudations when bruised, and *Cow Parsnip* has its eminently characteristic coarse leaves, which when once known cannot be later mistaken for anything else. It is only by a careful examination of the characteristics of individual species that headway can be made in the study of this order.

Araliaceæ.—The IVY is too familiar to need description. The berries, which appear in winter, are conspicuous in the absence of other fruits. They may be regarded as sub-poisonous, for though all manner of birds eat them with avidity and with no ill effects, they produce a vomiting sickness in children. A glucoside called *helixin* has been extracted from the berries, and it is to the presence of this substance that their bitter-sweet, quinine-like taste is due.

TABLE III

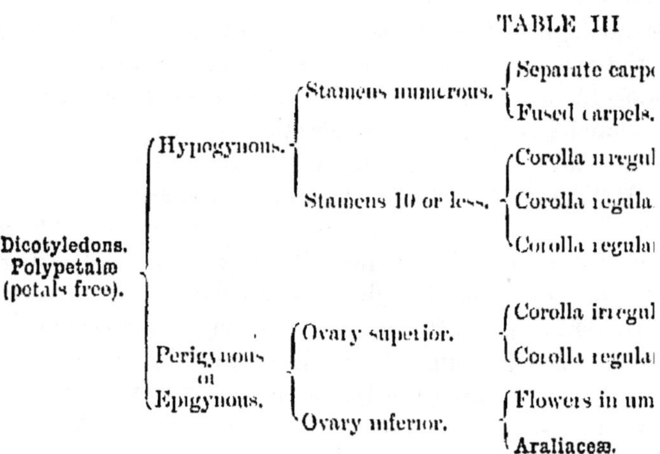

- **Dicotyledons. Polypetalæ** (petals free).
  - Hypogynous.
    - Stamens numerous.
      - Separate carp
      - Fused carpels.
    - Stamens 10 or less.
      - Corolla irregul
      - Corolla regula
      - Corolla regular
  - Perigynous or Epigynous.
    - Ovary superior.
      - Corolla irregul
      - Corolla regular
    - Ovary inferior.
      - Flowers in um
      - **Araliaceæ.**

CHAPTER VII

GAMOPETALÆ—I

Under this name are included all those plants the corolla of whose flowers is made up of 2, 4, or 5 fused petals. In some the union of petals is complete, but in others, as for example in the Cyclamen, the petals are joined only at the base. In both cases the plants are included in the Gamopetalæ. The flowers of this group readily divide themselves into two classes—those with a *superior* and those with an *inferior* ovary.

GAMOPETALOUS PLANTS WITH SUPERIOR OVARY

Scrophulariaceæ.—The Foxglove Family. This is an important order from the point of view of the present work. Normally the flowers possess 5 petals and 4 stamens. The pistil consists of 2 carpels joined together as shown in fig. 4, and the ovary in section has the appearance given in the same figure. This last point should be carefully noted, for it is the chief guide in distinguishing the Foxglove family from that of the Dead-nettle (Labiatæ).

FOXGLOVE (*Digitalis purpurea*).—A detailed description of this familiar plant is not necessary. All the garden varieties are derived from the wild plant by careful selection and breeding.

Poisonous Properties.—Many cases of poisoning have occurred from the leaves being eaten in mistake for the leaves of other plants, e.g. the Borage. Again, cases are on record in which poisoning results have followed the drinking, by ignorant people, of an infusion of "tea" made from the leaves of Foxglove. One case of homicide is recorded the poison having been administered to a patient by a homœopath. A fatal result followed the drinking, by a woman, of a large amount of the expressed juice of Foxglove leaves to relieve a swelling of

Fig. 60.—Foxglove (*Digitalis purpurea*)

the limbs. The symptoms of the poisoning are nausea, vomiting, and abdominal pains, followed by a remarkable slowing down of the pulse, and a feeling of faintness accompanied by slow respiration. All parts of the plant contain, among others, certain poisonous glucosides called *digitoxin* and *digitalin*, to the presence of which its physiological activities are due.

Medicinal Properties.—Although very poisonous, from the Foxglove is prepared a drug that is among the most valuable that we possess. When administered in small doses it induces a rise in the blood pressure of the arteries, and the heart contracts more powerfully and slowly. The drug has been appropriately called the "Pendulum of the Heart", since it diminishes undue or abnormal action of that organ and assists its driving power when that is deficient. The drug is also used in the treatment of dropsy and hæmorrhage.

Collection.—The National Herb-growing Association recommends that the following points be observed in collecting the leaves of Foxglove:—

1. That only the leaves of those plants which have flowered should be picked, and that discoloured leaves should be discarded.
2. That the stalks should be cut off, and the leaves placed on a floor having ample ventilation.
3. That the leaves should be placed singly, face downwards, and that both at night and when the weather is damp the windows should be closed.
4. That after two to four days the leaves should be placed in a warm place—for example, the rack of the kitchen stove—and kept there till dry and brittle.
5. That, finally, the leaves be placed in a tin or wooden box and kept in a dry place.

The following points should also be noted by collectors:—

1. Garden-planted Foxgloves are not so satisfactory as the wild forms.

2. The leaves rapidly deteriorate on keeping, and are worthless when more than a year old.
3. The second-year leaves are more active than those of the first year.

Present Source of Supply.—Digitalis was imported chiefly from France and Germany, but as the price has gone up from 23*s.*–33*s.* per cwt. to 92*s.* per cwt., the value of the plant has been greatly enhanced. Further, as the imported article is far inferior to carefully prepared leaves from the British plants, it seems as though in the near future there will be a boom in the cultivation of the Foxglove, as well as in the collection of the wild plants; and it is to be hoped that we shall before long be independent of the imported supplies.

Cultivation.—The plant is best cultivated in partial shade, as it demands only a moderate amount of sunshine. It grows best in a well-drained, loose soil, rich in leaf-mould. About 2 lb. of seed are required per acre. The seed is usually mixed with fine sand to secure even distribution. After sowing, it should be thinly covered with soil. The leaves are hand-picked in the second year, and a yield of from 1 to 2 tons is obtained per acre.

GREAT MULLEIN (*Verbascum Thapsus*).—This is a stout herbaceous stem reaching sometimes to a height of 5 or 6 feet, and easily distinguished by its *large flannel-like leaves* and club-shaped spikes of yellow flowers. It differs from the other members of the order in possessing 5 instead of 4 stamens.

The soft thick leaves boiled in milk and sweetened have been used as an emollient. The seeds, however, possess toxic properties, and children should not be allowed access to them. In the Middle Ages the Mullein enjoyed a great vogue as a curative for the troubles of the body and of the soul. To it was ascribed the power of driving away evil spirits, whilst on the material side it was used as a specific for many ailments. Great has been the fall of this plant. It is now chiefly employed as an adulterant, in substitution for Foxglove leaves.

There is a certain demand for Mullein flowers by herbalists, seeing that the flowers are imported from the Continent. In a leaflet issued by the Board of Agriculture and Fisheries, it is stated that "there will be a good inquiry for dry leaves".

FIGWORT (*Scrophularia nodosa*)—WATER FIGWORT (*Scrophularia aquatica*).—These two plants are common enough near rivers and in moist, shady spots. The flowers are very unusual in colour, being of a dingy greenish-purple hue. The general appearance of *S. nodosa* is given in fig. 61. The Water Figwort differs from this plant in having winged angles attached to the stem, otherwise the two are alike in almost every particular.

The name *Scrophularia* is interesting. It was given as a generic name to these plants, owing to the belief that they were effective as a cure for *scrofula*.

This genus gave its name to the order, and so we have Scrophulariaceæ. A crystalline bitter substance, to which the name *scrophularin* has been given, is extracted from the Figworts. This drug, taken internally, acts as an emetic and purgative. The whole genus must consequently be regarded with suspicion. Fortunately, animals will not touch these two plants. Needless to state, they have no value in the treatment of the disease which used to be known as *scrofulo*, and which is now regarded by med' ·l men as a form of tuberculosis. *Scrophularia nodosa* is, however, much in demand by herbalists.

The other members of Scrophulariaceæ may be dismissed in a few words. As a family the members produce acrid principles, bitter to the taste, and having a somewhat unpleasant smell; they present no temptation as edible plants, even to the most thoughtless. Thus TOADFLAX (*Linaria vulgaris*) is an acrid and poisonous

Fig. 61.—Figwort (*Scrophularia nodosa*)

a, Corolla opened. *b*, Calyx. *c*, Fruit (capsule).

plant, but there is no record against it. A crystalline bitter substance called *linarin* has been extracted from it, as well as two other substances, both of a pungent taste. Again, LOUSEWORT (*Pedicularis sylvatica*) is a familiar pasture plant. If taken internally it produces vomiting and purgative effects. Animals eat it only when the plant is young. Still another pasture plant is the COW-WHEAT (*Melampyrum pratense*) It is eaten by all animals while green; but it has been stated that if its seeds are present in any quantity in wheat-flour, the bread prepared from the flour is apt to produce giddiness when eaten.

The Labiatæ.—Dead-nettle Family. This is an important family which has no poisonous members, but which, on the contrary, includes a number of medicinal or sub-medicinal plants of great value. The identification of this order is not difficult. Like the Scrophulariaceæ, there are normally 5 sepals, 5 petals, and 4 stamens to each flower. The pistil, however, is totally different. If a glance be directed to the bottom of the tube formed by the petals, a circular disk divided into quadrants will be observed. From the centre of these rises a long style which terminates in a two-forked stigma (fig. 62, *a*). At the fruit stage, four little sub-globular nutlets can be observed (fig. 62, *b*). This type of pistil and fruit is formed only in one other Natural Order besides the Labiatæ, namely in the Boraginaceæ, from which they are easily distinguished. In addition, the Labiates have a square stem, and leaves arranged oppositely in pairs, each pair being set at right angles to the pair above it and to the pair below it.

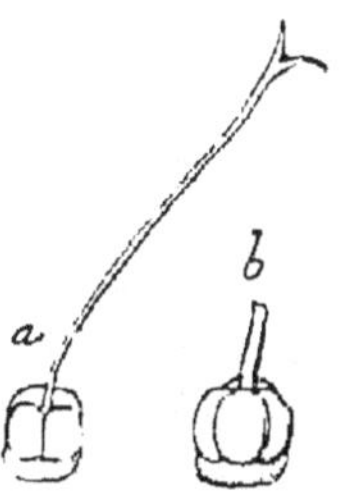

Fig 62.—*a*, Pistil of Labiatæ *b*, Fruit of Labiatæ

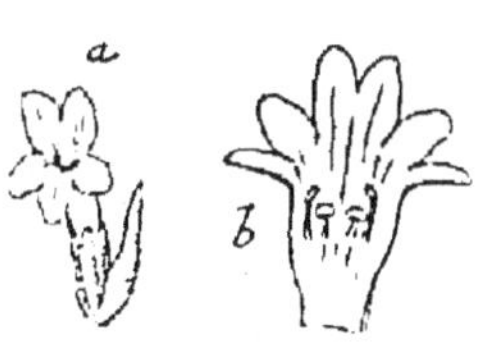

Fig 63.—*a*, Lavender Flower. *b*, Section of Corolla, Lavender

THE LAVENDERS.—The flower-heads of *Lavandula vera*, which compose Lavender, have too easily recognizable an odour to need a special description. The flower is shown in fig. 63, *a* and *b*. Although not a

British plant, Lavender is extensively cultivated for the market in this country, a volatile oil being produced by the distillation of the flowers. This Oil of Lavender is a pale-yellow liquid with a pungent taste. It is used as an aromatic stimulant and a carminative. It is an interesting fact that the English-grown Lavender oil is five to ten times more valuable than the French product. We may here direct attention to an obvious conclusion to be drawn from this fact—namely, that some foreign plants may be cultivated in this country with greater success than in their native country.

Another Lavender, namely the SPIKE LAVENDER (*Lavandula spica*), yields on distillation the *oil of spike lavender*. This possesses somewhat similar properties. though inferior, to the oil obtained from the Lavender mentioned above. Botanically, the Spike Lavender is distinguished from the former by the presence of *linear* bracts, those attached to the flowers of *Lavandula vera* being rhomboidal in shape.

Collection.—The flowers are picked when the lowermost ones have just appeared; they are stripped from the stalk and dried. The oil-glands are chiefly confined to the calyx, and appear on this structure (itself bluish-violet) as shining bodies, easily visible with the help of a pocket-lens.

Fig. 64.—Corolla, Mint Family

Mr. Shenstone points out that the demand for Continental lavender is normally three or four times that of the British variety because of the cheapness of the former. He suggests cultivating strains with a larger number of florets upon the spikes, and thus reducing the cost of production.

The Mint Family (*Mentha*)—The members of this essentially British family are distinguished from the other Labiates by the possession of the following characteristics:—

1. Their odour, at once pleasant and peculiar.
2. Their *corolla*, which is not bi-labiate (that is, two-lipped), but is nearly regular, and in length is scarcely larger than the calyx. Compare fig. 64 with fig. 63, which presents the *typical* labiate corolla.

Fig. 65.—Peppermint (*Mentha piperita*)

1, Corolla. 2, Corolla opened.

PEPPERMINT (*Mentha piperita*).—*Oil of Peppermint* is obtained by the distillation of fresh flowering Peppermint. The plant is often found wild in this country, but as an escape from cultivation. It is recognized by its oblong, smooth, lance-shaped, saw-edged leaves (fig. 65). The flowers are found in clusters, very close together at the top but interrupted below.

From the fresh flowers an oil is distilled which enters into the composition of peppermint-water, essence of peppermint, and spirit of peppermint. To many lay minds the name of peppermint is associated with noxious liquids which for their good they are sometimes compelled to swallow. Not only does peppermint mask the taste of such fluids, but it has a positive value as a stimulant and carminative; it also prevents griping in the intestinal canal. The most important constituent of Peppermint is *menthol or peppermint camphor*, a solid alcohol with the characteristic odour and taste of the oil.

Cultivation.—As before the War 40,000 cwt. were annually imported into this country from one district alone in Germany, and as the plant was formerly extensively grown at Mitcham, its cultivation should, at the present time, be a matter of interest. The plant grows in any ordinary good moist soil. It is propagated by division of roots or by cuttings in autumn or early spring. While the British variety is of better quality than the Continental, its high price seems to have brought about a decline in its sale.

SPEARMINT (*Mentha viridis*).—The special diagnostic features of this plant are the following:—

1. The leaves are *stalkless*, oblong-lanceolate, smooth on upper surface, and with a few hairs and glandular dots on the under surface: the edges are serrate (see fig. 66).
2. Each plant bears *several* slender spikes of flowers.
3. The flowers are of a lilac colour.

Fig. 66.—Spearmint (*Mentha viridis*)

a, Single flower.

Oil of Spearmint is obtained by a distillation of the fresh flowering plants.

CORN MINT (*Mentha arvensis*).—This is a very common plant in cornfields. It is best identified from the calyx, which is *bell-shaped*, and *which possesses triangular teeth as broad as they are long*. The leaves are stalked, ovate, and serrate (fig. 67). Although of high repute in former days, both from a culinary and

Fig. 67.—Leaf of Corn Mint (*Mentha arvensis*)

from a medicinal standpoint, at the present day its sole use is to furnish an ingredient in the preparation of *menthol.*

PENNYROYAL (*Mentha Pulegium*).—This is a valuable member of the Mint tribe, and can be identified by—

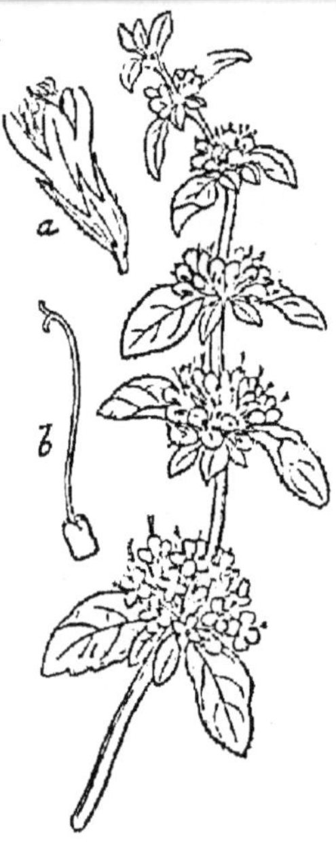

Fig 68.—Pennyroyal (*Mentha Pulegium*)

a, Corolla. *b*, Pistil.

1. Its stem, which is prostrate.
2. Its egg-shaped, nearly smooth leaves.
3. Its purple flowers in distant whorls.
4. Its smallness compared with others (it only reaches about 6 inches from the ground).

We often find Pennyroyal in cottage gardens, an infusion of the leaves being a favourite remedy against colds. It was more valued officially in former days than it is now, though its volatile oil (the *oleum pulegii* of the pharmacists) is still largely used. The herb is in steady demand, and is largely cultivated in this country. A large amount of the plant was also imported before the War. The volatile oil supplies a stimulant and an emmenagogue.

There are altogether eight Mints in this country, and the following classification may help to distinguish the four noted above from the remaining four.

Mints.

- Throat of calyx devoid of hairs.
  - Flowers in heads at ends of stalks.
    - Leaves stalkless, or only lower ones stalked.
      - Round
      - Silky le
      - Smooth
    - Leaves stalked.
      - Spikes.
      - Hairy 1
  - Flowers in whorls in axils of leaves.
    - Teeth of calyx devoid of hairs. = MA
    - Teeth of calyx hairy. = COR
- Throat of calyx hairy. = PENNYROYAL.

Cultivation of Mint.—Spearmint, the variety mostly in request for culinary purposes, is easily grown in good, rather moist soil. Propagation is effected by division of the clumps in early spring. The clumps are set about 9 inches apart. The cultivation of Peppermint may be accomplished in the same way. It is advisable to water the beds well in dry weather, and to top-dress with fresh soil once a year.

Fig. 69.—White Horehound (*Marrubium vulgare*)
a, Corolla opened. *b*, Flower. *c*, Calyx showing hooked teeth

WHITE HOREHOUND (*Marrubium vulgare*).—The leaves and tops of the White Horehound are used to make a syrup which is extensively employed in making up cough mixtures. The outstanding features of the plant are the following:—

1. The whole plant is covered with a *woolly down.*
2. The leaves are wrinkled.
3. The flowers are small and white.
4. The *ten* calyx-teeth are sharp and *hooked* (fig. 69).

This herb contains a bitter crystalline principle called *marrubin,* also a little *volatile oil* and *tannin.*

The Board of Agriculture and Fisheries (Leaflet 288) states that it might pay to cultivate Horehound, as it is in steady demand. It grows wild in this country in waste grounds, but is not common. For its cultivation ordinary garden soil will serve the purpose, propagation being effected by cuttings and root-division, for the herb is a hardy perennial.

White Horehound is used as a remedy for coughs and pulmonary complaints generally.

Wild Marjoram (*Origanum vulgare*).—In our gardens there are about twenty-five species of herbaceous perennials that are included under the genus Origanum. The only British species, however, is the Wild Marjoram. This grows wild in dry, bushy places, especially on chalk or limestone. The herb has egg-shaped, downy leaves (fig. 70), a head of purple flowers, and *a collection of bracts which are longer than the flowers and tinged with the same colour.*

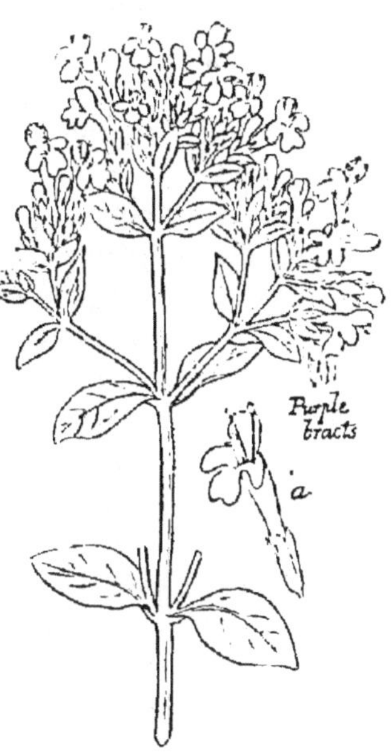

Fig. 70—Wild Marjoram (*Origanum vulgare*)

a, Corolla.

This plant is usually cultivated as a pot-herb, but is also used medicinally as a *stimulant* and a *carminative.* It yields about 2 per cent of volatile oil.

The cultivation of Marjoram may be effected by seeds, or by cuttings of the young flowerless shoots, or by root-division.

There is a steady demand for the plant, which can be grown easily in cottage gardens.

ROSEMARY (*Rosmarinus officinalis*).—This old-fashioned plant, which forms a dense bush about 4 feet high, is not a native of Britain, although it is cultivated in the South of England. The leaves are stalkless, grey, and about an inch long, pungently aromatic, and somewhat camphoraceous. They are gathered for the production of oil of rosemary. The oil is a slight stimulant, and formerly was extensively used to relieve headache and mental weariness, possibly also to hide from the curious an indulgence in sack, Canary, and Malvoisie. Did not Dame Margery cover her weakness by stoutly declaring that the odour from her still-room at curfew was due to Rosemary? At the present day the herb is employed as a stimulant, but only for external use, its usefulness in this respect being well established; consequently we find Rosemary figuring largely in hair-washes. Internally it is now very rarely given. It is also used as a preservative in making candied fruit.

The plant flourishes best in a light sandy loam in a well-drained sunny position. It does not figure in Mr. Holmes's lists of plants in request by herbalists.

THYME. *Thymus Serpyllum* (WILD THYME), *Thymus vulgaris* (GARDEN THYME).—There is only one native species, namely the Wild Thyme, a little plant with a much-branched woody stem and small fringed leaves, surmounted by numerous heads of purple flowers (fig. 71). It is common in dry, heathy places, its presence in hot weather being perceptible at some distance owing to its fragrant odour. The herb is used as a stimulant and for curing flatulency, but there seems now to be no market for it. The *oil of thyme*, so much used for the production of the antiseptic *thymol*, is obtained from a species native to South Europe called *Thymus vulgaris*.

This species, however, is cultivated in this country, and whilst most of the oil in commerce comes from France, the best is obtained from British-grown varieties of the same plant. There is, in addition, a demand by herbalists for LEMON THYME (*Thymus citriodorus*), another non-British species, which is included by Mr. Hosking in his list of hardy herbs used in medicine.

Fig. 71.—Wild Thyme (*Thymus Serpyllum*)
a, Corolla opened. *b*. Calyx and stigma

SAGE.—The *Salvia officinalis* of the pharmacists is not a native plant, although grown in our gardens. The genus Salvia is distinguished from all Labiates by possessing *only 2 stamens* instead of the usual complement of 4. A garden plant with the Labiate characteristics and only 2 stamens may safely be regarded as a species of the genus Salvia. The leaves of *S. officinalis* are thick, greyish-green, wrinkled, soft, and hairy. They have a bitter taste, and are aromatic and somewhat astringent. A volatile oil is obtained from them which is used as a stimulant and an astringent.

For the cultivation of the plant, seeds or cuttings may be used; it grows best in rich loam to which decayed vegetable matter has been added.

Sage in quantity is in demand by the herbalists on account of its astringent and aromatic properties.

BALM (*Melissa officinalis*).—Balm is a common perennial herb, the leaves of which possess a distinctive aromatic odour.

The chief characteristics of the plant are the following:—

1. The flowers are white.
2. The flowers are arranged in whorls.
3. The calyx is tubular and 5-toothed.
4. The leaves are ovate, about 2 inches long, somewhat hairy and glandular.

This herb is sometimes used in the making of claret cup, and an infusion made by boiling the leaves in water is an old-fashioned remedy for colds. A volatile oil, extracted from the leaves and flower tops, is used medicinally as a stimulant and to correct flatulency. There is a great demand for Balm by perfumers and by herbalists. It can be cultivated in any fairly good garden soil, and propagation can be effected by cuttings and by root-divisions in spring.

The above plants of the Labiatæ do not include all the wild flowers of this family which at one time or another have been used medicinally. Among others are: BASIL (*Ocymum Basilicum*), HYSSOP (*Hyssopus officinalis*), BUGLE (*Ajuga reptans*), BLACK HOREHOUND (*Ballota nigra*), WHITE DEAD-NETTLE (*Lamium album*), YELLOW ARCHANGEL (*Lamium Galeobdolon*), MOTHERWORT (*Leonurus Cardiaca*), CATMINT (*Nepeta Cataria*), GROUND IVY (*Nepeta hederacea*), SELF-HEAL (*Prunella vulgaris*), CLARY (*Salvia Sclarea*), SAVORY (*Saturreia montana*), SKULL-CAP (*Scutellaria lateriflora*); the various species of *Stachys* like WOUNDWORT and WOOD BETONY; species of *Teucrium* like WOOD SAGE. It will be seen from this list that, in the past, considerable attention was bestowed on the order Labiatæ by the followers of Æsculapius: no doubt the strong aroma which many members of this family possess would attract attention and suggest the possibilities of medicinal virtues. Further, in "faith" cures a good aroma is an asset of great value, and there can be little doubt that our predecessors made great use of psychological factors in their treatment of disease. In the lists of plants supplied to herbalists the Labiates are very strongly represented.

Ericaceæ.—The Heath Family. In this order are included some plants, like the Ling or Heather, which cover large tracts of country. These are, fortunately, not of a poisonous nature. To the same family belong the Rhododendron, Bilberry, Whortleberry, and Cranberry.

In the flowers the calyx is mostly wanting or very insignificant. The corolla is composed of 4 or 5 fused petals. The stamens are either 5 or 10 in number when the corolla is made up of 5 petals, or are 4 or 8 in number when the flower has 4 petals. The pistil is composed of 4 or 5 fused carpels.

In the Gamopetalæ the stamens are attached to the corolla. It is very useful to remember that in the Ericaceæ *the stamens are quite unconnected with the corolla* A knowledge of this fact helps considerably in facilitating the identification of the order.

RHODODENDRON.—Among the poisonous plants of the Ericaceæ must be reckoned the Rhododendron (including under this term the Azalea), many species of which are in cultivation. The genus is not British, but it can scarcely nowadays be omitted from a study of British plants, owing to the universal distribution of its members throughout the British Isles. All of these possess acrid narcotic properties. The honey which is secreted from a species of AZALEA (*A. pontica*), a plant very common in Asia Minor, is stated to have caused the distemper which seized Xenophon's soldiers in the retreat of the Ten Thousand. The soldiers became intoxicated after eating a small quantity of the honey, while a large quantity made them mad. There can be little doubt that those properties, which the tropical species possess in an acute degree, are to be found in a milder form also in the species which grow in a temperate climate. Death is known to have resulted after eating the flesh of hares which had fed on *Rhododendron chrysanthum*.

Kalmia latifolia is a hardy evergreen shrub from N. America, and is comparatively common in our gardens. The flowers are very ornamental, and may be recognized by the markedly peculiar stamens, which are *bent down and thrust into little pockets in the corolla*. The whole plant is dangerous, the leaves in particular being acrid and narcotic. There are records of death having ensued after eating birds (pheasants, partridges, &c.) which had fed on the buds and seeds of this plant; the birds themselves being immune to the poison.

LABRADOR TEA (*Ledum latifolium*).—This is a hardy evergreen shrub, from which, as its name implies, a "tea" is prepared. A certain amount of risk attends the drinking of this infusion, headache and nausea often resulting therefrom.

MARSH TEA (*Ledum palustre*).—This is very similar to the preceding, and belongs to the same genus. Its properties are the same, but it is also used medicinally on account of the *tannin*, *volatile oil*, &c., which it contains. Preparations from this plant are employed in the treatment of dysentery and certain cutaneous diseases.

BEARBERRY (*Arctostaphylos Uva-ursi*).—The most important member of the Ericaceæ from a medicinal point of view is the Bearberry, which is recognized by the following characteristics:—

1. The plant is a small shrub, with prostrate stems and egg-shaped, entire, evergreen leaves.
2. The leaves turn red in autumn.
3. The fruit consists of small red berries.

The dried leaves contain 6 to 7 per cent of *tannin*, also *gallic acid*, a glucoside called *arbutin*, as well as other principles. Arbutin is very bitter, and is decomposed by acids into *glucose* and *hydroquinone*. The leaves of Bearberry are in demand because of their astringent, *tonic*, and *diuretic* purposes.

CHAPTER VIII

GAMOPETALÆ—II

Primulaceæ.—The Primrose Family. The student should study the primrose flower very carefully, in order

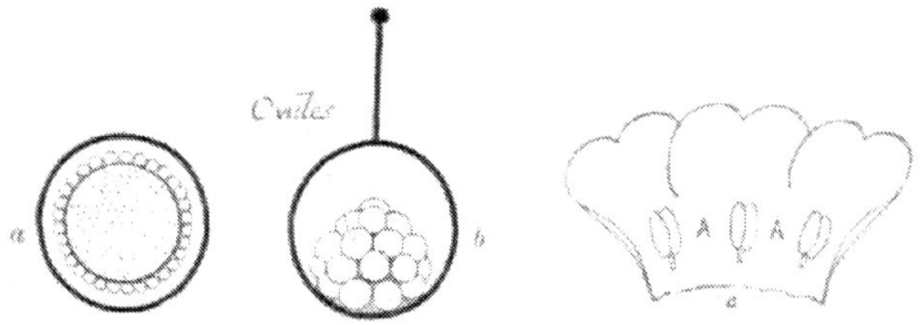

Fig. 72.—*a*, Model of Ovary of Primrose. *b*, Ripe Ovary, Primulaceæ. *c*, Position of Stamens in Primulaceæ.

to understand the characteristics of the Primulaceæ. In particular, the ripe ovary should be examined; this will be seen to conform to the type shown in fig. 72, *b*. It consists of one cavity, from the base of which arises a solid round mass of tissue (the placenta), on which are placed the numerous ovules which the ovary contains. We may make, in imagination, a model of the ovary by placing a golf-ball inside a hollow rubber ball, and then plastering the golf-ball with fairly large round bullets. A section through such a model across the middle would present the same appearance as fig. 72, *a*. The whole order presents, in addition, a peculiarity of arrangement in the flower which is very helpful for diagnosing purposes, namely, the position of the stamens, which are placed *opposite* to, and not *alternate* with, the petals (fig. 72, *c*). In most flowers the stamens are inserted in the position marked A in the diagram, that is, between the petals.

All the species are herbaceous, most of the members being forms of lowly growth. The sepals are joined and so are the petals. The number of parts is usually 5, but sometimes 4.

Primula Group.—This comprises the familiar WILD PRIMROSE (*Primula vulgaris*), the COWSLIP (*Primula veris*), OXLIP (*Primula elatior*), and others. Of the many cultivated varieties of the genus Primula, the JAPANESE PRIMROSE (*Primula obconica*) is the only one which has to be handled with care, as its juice affects the skin, producing a form of Urticaria, prominent patches and wheals appearing; sometimes the hands swell and are very painful.

From Cowslip is made a pleasant soporific wine. The flowers are in great demand by herbalists, but hitherto they have been imported, the plant being doubtless considered not worth collecting in this country.

In the Alps the leaves of AURICULA (*Primula Auricula*) are used as a remedy for coughs.

CYCLAMEN (*Cyclamen* sp.).—It is easy to distinguish a Cyclamen from the rest of the Primulaceæ, because of the appearance of the petals; these are wheel-shaped, with the lobes turned back (see fig. 73). There is one wild species (*C. hederifolium*) which is growing in Sussex and Kent, which has pink flowers and spotted heart-shaped leaves. In the gardens there are several different species and varieties, all of which possess the peculiar reflexed corolla characteristic of the genus. Henslow states that the tubers of the *Cyclamen Persicum*—the different varieties of which are cultivated in our country in gardens—are eaten by swine. Be that as it may, these tubers contain an active principle called *cyclamin*, which on being acted on by acids gives *cyclamiretin*, an extremely poisonous substance. Sometimes the tubers have been used medicinally — presumably by unqualified practitioners — and have produced violent results, acting both as a purgative and as an emetic. The juice, extracted from the tubers, kills small fish when mixed in the water in the proportion of only 1 in 3000.

Fig 73.—Flower of Cyclamen

SCARLET PIMPERNEL or POOR MAN'S WEATHER-GLASS (*Anagallis arvensis*).—This is a pretty little prostrate plant with scarlet flowers, often found in cultivated ground. The seeds have on occasion been given to cage-birds, in mistake for seeds of chickweed, with fatal results

Gentianaceæ.—There are no specially distinctive features common to the members of this family by which the Natural Order can be recognized. The following features are common to most of the members of the group:—

1. The leaves are stalkless and opposite
2. The calyx and corolla are 4–10-lobed.

3. The stamens *alternate* with the petals (compare Primulaceæ).
4. The ovary is superior.

Bitter principles predominate in the members of this order, so that we find them used as tonics, among which they rank very high.

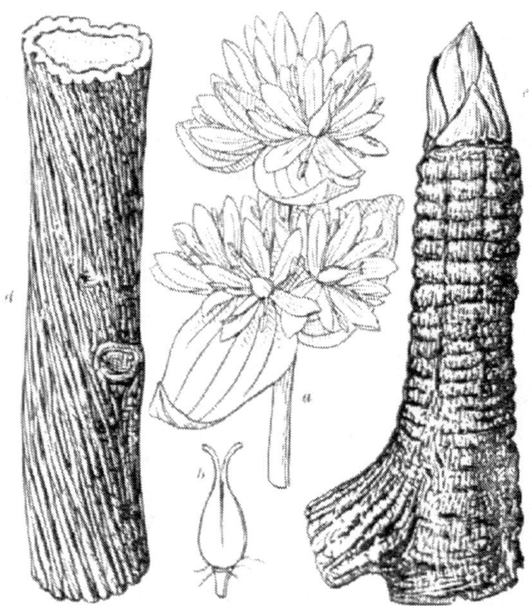

Fig. 74.—Yellow Gentian (*Gentiana lutea*)

a, Upper part of flower spike. *b*, Fruit. *c*, Part of rhizome. *d*, Part of root.

YELLOW GENTIAN (*Gentiana lutea*).—Although a native of Central and Southern Europe, this plant grows readily in this country. It reaches from 2 to 4 feet in height, and forms yellow flowers in July. The dried rhizome and roots furnish one of the most widely used tonic-bitters. The Swiss and Tyrolese use the rhizome to manufacture a "gentian brandy" which is much prized as a stomachic and stimulant. The active principles of the rhizome have been determined: they are certain glucosides, which have been also found in some of the other members of this family.

Common Centaury (*Erythræa Centaurium*).—Glucosides with properties similar to those found in Yellow Gentian have been extracted from the Common Centaury, the latter being occasionally substituted for the Yellow Gentian. The points of recognition are the following:—

1. The stem is erect, square, and branched, terminating above in tufts of rose-coloured flowers.
2. The leaves are oblong, with strong parallel ribs (fig. 75).
3. The flowers expand only in fine weather.

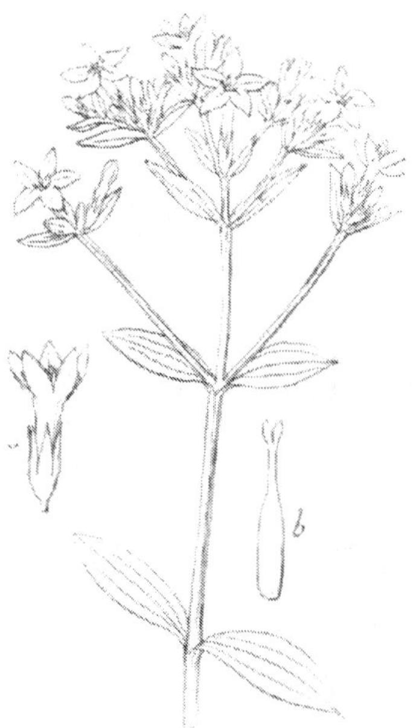

Fig. 75.—Common Centaury (*Erythræa Centaurium*)

a, Single flower. *b*, Pistil.

The bitterness of this plant is due to a substance called *erythro-centaurin*; so great is the bitterness of the root that the old herbalists called it *earth-gall*. It grows readily in rockeries, and prefers light soil, propagation being usually effected by seeds sown in spring. As may be supposed, the Centaury is a great stand-by to the herbalists, and is in demand by them in very large quantities.

BOG-BEAN or BUCK-BEAN (*Menyanthes trifoliata*).—This dweller in the marshes is easily recognized.

1. The large ternate leaves have a distinctive character: the stem is overtopped by large leaves each composed of three leaflets (fig. 76).
2. The flowers in bud are of a bright rose-colour, but appear white when fully expanded, the inner surface of the petals being white. Further, *each petal has an elegant fringe of white filaments.*

Fig 76.—Bog-bean (*Menyanthes trifoliata*)

a, Section of capsule showing seeds. b, Ovary and style, with calyx-teeth below.

The medicinal value of Bog-bean leaves is very great, as they are bitter without being astringent; the bitterness is due to the presence of a glucoside called *menyanthin*. It is said that 2 oz. of dried leaves are equivalent to 1 lb. of hops for brewing purposes. Medicinally the Bog-bean is employed as a *tonic* and a *purgative*.

Before the War we imported about 5 tons of the plant, the bulk coming from Germany; as this source is now cut off, the present supplies come from English and Irish sources. Its price to-day is more than treble what it was before the War, when it fetched about 20s. a cwt. The leaves are collected in spring or early summer.

Boraginaceæ.—The Comfrey Family. Most of the members composing the Boraginaceæ possess large, rough, hairy leaves and blue or purple flowers; in all cases the leaves are very large in comparison with the flowers. The question as to whether a certain flower showing these characteristics does or does not belong to the Boraginaceæ can be definitely settled by an examination of the pistil. This organ is of practically the same structure as in the Labiatæ (fig. 77), this particular type being exclusively confined to these two Natural Orders. The flower has normally 5 fused sepals, 5 fused petals, and 5 stamens. As the flowers of Labiatæ have only 4 stamens, and have an irregular corolla, the two orders are readily distinguished from each other. The species included under the Boraginaceæ possess soft mucilaginous juices, which added to beverages impart to these a refreshing taste. There are no poisonous plants in the order, but a few have a medicinal or sub-medicinal interest.

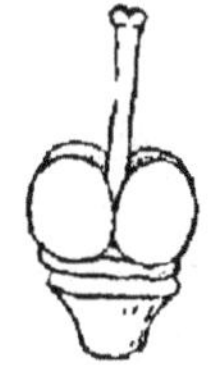

Fig 77.—Pistil of Boraginaceæ

Comfrey (*Symphytum officinale*).—This handsome plant, with its yellow, pink or purple, drooping flowers, and large, elliptical, hairy, pointed leaves, is common in watery places and on the banks of rivers. Another striking feature are the wings which line the upper part of the stem.

The root of Comfrey is in great demand, the plant being regularly cultivated, as herbalists use the roots extensively. Comfrey has long been used as an old-fashioned, domestic cough-remedy.[1]

[1] The chief constituent of the root is *mucilage*, others being *tannin* and *starch*. The leaves are sometimes grown as an esculent vegetable, but are little valued except as food for horses.

The cultivation of the herb is a very easy matter, and in many cases the difficulty is to prevent it from spreading over the whole garden, after it has once got a good start; the smallest bit of root left in the ground will grow, and raise a fresh colony. The leaves are collected in May, and the roots in July.

ALKANET or BUGLOSS (*Anchusa*).—The Alkanet root of the pharmacists is the dried root of *Anchusa tinctoria*, a native of Southern Europe and Hungary. The two British representatives are the EVERGREEN ALKANET (*Anchusa sempervirens*) and the COMMON ALKANET (*Anchusa officinalis*). They are not used medicinally, but a red substance is extracted from them which is used as a dye.

Convolvulaceæ.—The Bindweed Family. Of very little importance. Most of the members of this family have an acrid taste, and exude a milky fluid when bruised; cattle will not touch the plants. Taken internally they act as purgatives.

Solanaceæ.—The Potato Family. This is an extremely important family, embracing in its fold some of the deadliest of poisonous plants, some of the most valuable of medicinal plants, and likewise some which provide the most nutritious of foods.

The identification of the order is best attained by carefully following the rules for guidance set forth on p. 151. A plant with fused petals, a superior ovary, and a regular corolla is either a member of the Solanaceæ or of the Convolvulaceæ. As all the species included in the latter order are either twining or prostrate herbs, it is not difficult to distinguish between these two orders.

There are three genera indigenous to this country, all of which call for careful consideration:—

1. *Solanum*. The Nightshade.
2. *Atropa*. The Deadly Nightshade.
3. *Hyoscyamus*. The Henbane.

Fig. 78.—Woody Nightshade or Bittersweet (*Solanum Dulcamara*)

a, Stamen.
b, Pistil.
c, Fruit.

Fig. 79.—Black Nightshade (*Solanum nigrum*)

a, Pistil.
b, Stamen.

Solanum:—

(i) Woody Nightshade or Bittersweet (*S. Dulcamara*).
(ii) Black Nightshade (*S. nigrum*).
(iii) Potato (*Solanum tuberosum*)

The Woody Nightshade (*S. Dulcamara*) has a shrubby, climbing stem, heart-shaped leaves, and drooping flowers. It climbs among bushes, forming *purple flowers with yellow anthers* (fig. 78). Later, the flowers are succeeded by scarlet berries (fig. 78). The name BITTERSWEET is due to the fact that the taste of the stem is at first bitter and then becomes sweet. The plant is poisonous in all its parts; on several occasions children have died from having eaten the berries. These are more poisonous when green than when ripe. A poisonous narcotic alkaloid called *solanine* and a poisonous glucoside called *dulcamarin* have been extracted from the plant; it is the latter which is responsible for the bittersweet taste. Medicinally the plant is used as a mild narcotic, young branches two or three years old being employed for this purpose. They are cut in autumn and then dried.

The BLACK NIGHTSHADE (*S. nigrum*) is a smaller plant, about 18 inches high; it exhales a disagreeable odour, and its flower forms purple-black globular berries. Like the preceding, it forms the poisonous *solanine*. It is on record that three children who had eaten the fruit suffered from dilated pupils, nausea, colic, and convulsions.

THE POTATO (*Solanum tuberosum*).—Although not indigenous to Britain, the Potato has been with us so long that for practical purposes it must be regarded as a native plant. It came originally from Chile, being introduced into this country in 1586 by Sir Walter Raleigh. It is not widely known that the leaves and berries of the Potato are narcotic, and that even the useful tuber is not always free from poison. As the latter, however, resides near the surface, and as it is destroyed by the operation of cooking, there is very little danger to be apprehended. A tuber contains more of the poison if it has lain near or on the surface and has become somewhat green in colour. The advent of "new" potatoes into a house is sometimes followed by a visit from the doctor, and accidents to animals fed on potato-peelings are by no means uncommon; in the latter case,

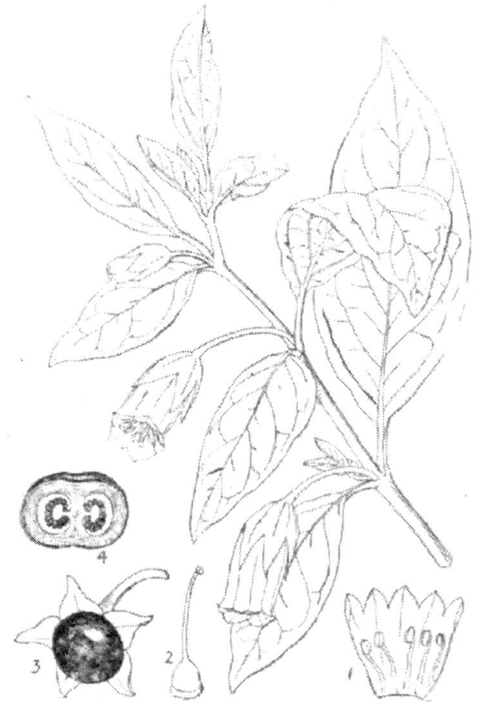

Fig. 80.—Deadly Nightshade (*Atropa Belladonna*)

1, Corolla opened. 2, Pistil. 3, Fruit. 4, Section of fruit.

poisoning effects are observed only when the animals have been fed on the uncooked peelings.

Deadly Nightshade (*Atropa Belladonna*).—There is no plant in Great Britain which is more in request for medicinal purposes at the present than the Belladonna. It is found growing as a stout herbaceous plant, forming dingy, purple, bell-shaped flowers, which later form large, black, shining berries of attractive appearance (fig. 80).

Poisonous Properties.—The berries are intensely sweet, very attractive in appearance, and extremely poisonous. With such a combination of properties it is scarcely a matter of surprise that numerous fatal mishaps have occurred. The berries, however, are the least poisonous, the most active form of the poison being found in the root. To add still further to the element of danger, drying does not seem to alter the active properties of the poison. Henslow records that at the beginning of last century 150 soldiers suffered at one time after eating the berries of this plant; and it was undoubtedly the berries of Belladonna which were eaten by the soldiers of Mark Antony, and which caused them to lose their memory and become insane. Recently a young woman was brought to hospital after having, when drunk, swallowed nearly an ounce of "eye-drops" (4 grains atropine sulphate to the ounce). The face was flushed, the lips were dry and blistered, whilst the pupils were widely dilated and immobile. She became delirious, but ultimately recovered. In some cases, even an external application of a belladonna plaster has been known to produce fatal results; the writer in his own person can record a case which very nearly proved fatal.

From the root the powerful alkaloid *atropine* is obtained. It forms silky, prismatic, needle-like crystals, which have a bitter, burning taste.

Medicinal Properties.—Belladonna is used for dilating the pupils, and also as a sedative, narcotic, and anti-hydrotic.

Distribution.—The herb grows on most soils, but is partial to a chalky or a limestone soil; often found growing near ruins. Though found as a rare plant in a few Scottish counties, from Westmorland southwards its occurrence is comparatively common.

Collection.—The leaf and stem may be collected at any season, as there is no marked variation in the amount of alkaloids found in them; the root only shows a small seasonal variation.

Present Source of Supply.—It is important at this juncture to direct attention to this and the following section, as there will be a shortage of these plants for the next three or four years. Before the War, the bulk of the world's supply came from South Hungary. Only a little Belladonna root is dug in England. The stocks had become short even before the present War, on account of the interference with cultivation caused by the Balkan War of 1912–13. The Board of Agriculture and Fisheries reports that the root, which realized 45*s.* per cwt. in January, 1914, was sold for 65*s.* in June of the same year, and on the outbreak of war it rose at once to 100*s.*, and at the end of August fetched 150*s.* Again, Belladonna *leaves* from abroad, sold at 45*s.* to 50*s.* a cwt. before the War, were unobtainable at the end of August, 1914, at 1*s.* per lb. The annual consumpt in this country is about 50 tons, but much more is required for export purposes.

Cultivation.—The seeds germinate slowly. These are drilled in rows 3 feet apart, and 2–3 lb of seed are used to the acre. In addition, it is customary to grow the plant in seed-beds so as to fill in gaps due to dormant seeds and other causes. Being liable to injury, the seedlings receive a light top-dressing of farmyard manure to preserve young shoots. The plants are kept 18 inches apart the first year, and by September they attain a height of 1½–2½ feet from the ground. It is the leaves of these plants which are collected. Before winter, the stalks left after the collection are thinned till they are

$2\frac{1}{2}$-3 feet apart. In the second year the English crop is cut while flowering in June, and is usually carted straight to the factory in which the extract is made.

The average crop of fresh herb in the second and third years is 5 to 6 tons per acre. A second crop is obtained in September in good seasons. In the fourth year the root is collected, washed, and sliced to accelerate drying.

Heavy rainfall and lack of sunshine are responsible for occasional disasters in the cultivation of Belladonna.

Mr. Shenstone has reminded us that, inasmuch as the value of Belladonna and similar plants depends entirely on their alkaloidal contents, co-operation between the grower and the chemist is desirable, if we wish to cultivate plants of high alkaloidal value.

HENBANE (*Hyoscyamus niger*).—This is another of our poisonous plants which is also of great medicinal importance. It can be identified without much difficulty.

1. The corolla is yellowish, with veins of a violet tint; it is, further, funnel-shaped and about an inch or more in diameter (fig. 81).
2. The leaves are large, hairy, and viscid.
3. The whole plant has a very disagreeable smell.
4. The flowers are arranged in rows all along one side of the stem.

The fruit is a 2-celled capsule and is enveloped by the calyx.

Poisonous Properties.—Every part of the plant is poisonous; the root is the most prolific source of trouble, as it may be, and has been frequently, mistaken for the root of parsnip or of chicory; the seeds have been eaten by children. The poison is not affected by boiling or drying, and is therefore all the more to be feared. As a rule, animals refuse to eat the plant. Henslow records that the whole of the inmates of a monastery were poisoned, after partaking of the root in mistake for chicory: the monks suffered from hallucinations, and rang the bell for matins at midnight. The active principles are two alkaloids, called *hyoscyamine* and *hyoscine*, both powerful narcotics; and these are more effective, or present in greater quantity, at the time when the seeds are ripening.

Fig 81 —Henbane (*Hyoscyamus niger*)

a, Capsule, with lid opening and seeds falling out *b*, Lower part of corolla opened out.

Medicinal Properties—An extract from the leaves is used in medicine, and produces the effect of opium without the disagreeable after-results which follow the administration of that drug. In some parts of the country the seeds and capsules of Henbane are smoked like tobacco as a remedy for toothache; but the practice is dangerous, and sometimes results in convulsions and temporary insanity. It is not surprising to find that this plant, in the Middle Ages, was one of the "witches'" herbs.

Distribution.—It is found in sandy waste places from Dumbarton southwards; it is not native to Scotland: in Ireland it is very common.

Collection.—The official leaves of the British Pharmacopœia are the leaves and flowering tops of second-year plants of the biennial Henbane, whilst the dry commercial leaves that were imported from Germany and Russia are derived from the wild annual plants.

Present Source of Supply.—We are officially informed that there will be for some time a demand for leaves at an enhanced price. The normal price of the Continental drug is 40*s.* to 45*s.* per cwt. The English-grown plant is ordinarily worth 3*s.* to 6*s.* a lb. At present the demand is being met by the established drug-farms. Our annual requirement is 20–25 tons for home use, but much more is required for export purposes.

Cultivation.—The seed of the annual variety is sown in rows 18 inches apart, and those of the biennial variety 2–2½ feet apart. The seeds are collected just before the capsule which contains them opens. In a pamphlet of the National Herb-Growing Association it is suggested that, by cutting off the flowering tops, and allowing only six capsules on each plant to come to maturity, strong seed will be produced which will probably yield biennial Henbane.

Thorn Apple (*Datura Stramonium*).—This is another valuable but poisonous plant, which appears occasionally on dunghills and waste grounds, and which, though not British, may for all practical purposes be regarded as such. Its value at the present time is attested by the fact that in a leaflet issued by the Board of Agriculture and Fisheries (Leaflet 288) prominence is given to the mode of cultivation best suited for this plant.

The leaves are large, wavy, and have a toothed margin; the flowers are about *three inches* long, and white in colour. The capsular fruits are covered with spines, and when ripe split into 4 valves, leaving a portion at the centre upon which are borne several rough seeds of a black colour. When bruised the plant gives forth an offensive smell. From the young leaves, collected when the plant is in flower, is obtained an extract, which contains *atropine*, *hyoscyamine*, and *hyoscine*, which is used for purposes similar to those for which Belladonna is employed.

Stramonium leaves are used in the preparation of asthma powders and of medicinal cigarettes.

Collection.—The leaves are removed in late summer while the plant is still flowering. They are dried as quickly as possible. The capsules are gathered from plants allowed to stand. They are allowed to split and shed their seed.

Present Source of Supply.—Usually imported from Hungary and Germany, there is naturally a dearth at the present time. The normal price of foreign Stramonium leaves is about 40*s*. a cwt.; this price has now been more than doubled.

Cultivation.—The seeds are drilled in rows about 2 feet apart, about 10 to 15 lb. being used to the acre. The plant grows well in sunny situations.

CHAPTER IX

GAMOPETALÆ—III

GAMOPETALOUS PLANTS WITH INFERIOR OVARY

Campanulaceæ.—The only plants of interest to us in this order are the familiar LOBELIAS that figure so largely in garden borders. All Lobelias exude an acrid juice when bruised which produces internal effects in the human body of the same nature as does Belladonna. One of the plants of this order, the INDIAN TOBACCO (*Lobelia inflata*), a native of N. America, is used for asthma, but is dangerously emetic and narcotic. In one recorded case, death resulted thirty-six hours after a sufferer had taken a dose of this plant on the advice of a quack practitioner. *Lobelia urens* has intense blistering properties, and it is well to issue a warning against the whole group of members classed under the genus Lobelia.

The Compositæ.—Daisy and Dandelion Family. We pass now to the most highly developed among all the families of the vegetable kingdom. It is also the most successful in point of numbers, for it far outstrips all other orders in the number of genera in the order, and the number of species in the genus. One has only to think of the Daisy or of the Dandelion to realize that the number of individuals in the species may also be very large.

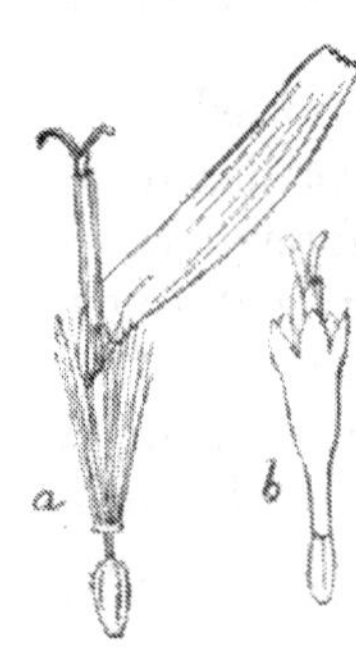

Fig. 82.—*a*, Ray Floret of Daisy, *b*, Disk Floret of the same

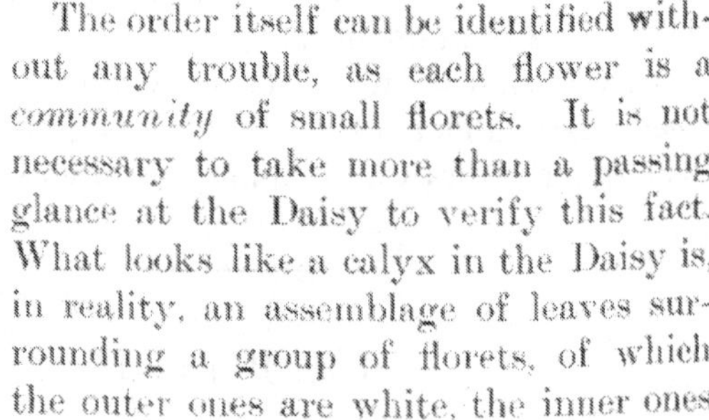

The order itself can be identified without any trouble, as each flower is a *community* of small florets. It is not necessary to take more than a passing glance at the Daisy to verify this fact. What looks like a calyx in the Daisy is, in reality, an assemblage of leaves surrounding a group of florets, of which the outer ones are white, the inner ones orange-coloured. These two types of florets are shown in fig. 82, which should be studied in conjunction with the flower itself. The only other order with which the Compositæ can be confused is the *Dipsaceæ*. In the latter, however, the stamens are *free*; whilst in the Composite flower they are *fused*, and form a ring round the style. Whilst the order can be easily recognized, its various species are not so easily identified, and great care must be given to the examination of the characteristics peculiar to each species.

A *bitterness* of taste is found in a large number of the Compositæ; some possess aromatic secretions, whilst others exude a milky narcotic juice when they are bruised. As there are 109 species in Great Britain, it is remarkable that there should be no poisonous plants of any consequence among them. In some form or other,

Fig. 83.—Mugwort (*Artemisia vulgaris*)

Fig. 84.—Wormwood (*Artemisia Absinthium*)

over 40 of these have come at one time or other within the province of medical practitioners, qualified and otherwise.

WORMWOOD (*Artemisia* sp.).—Of this group MUGWORT (*Artemisia vulgaris*) is the commonest. The root is a stimulant and tonic, and at one time was much used as a remedy for epilepsy. A volatile oil, an acrid resin, and tannin have been extracted from the root. In some country districts a "tea" is made from Mugwort root, the beverage being held to be a remedy for rheumatism. The following points suffice for the identification of Mugwort:—

1. The florets are brownish-yellow.
2. The leaves are white and woolly on the under side, but green on the upper side (fig. 83).
3. The stem is furrowed, and about 2–4 feet high.
4. The whole plant has a pleasant aroma.

It is not surprising to find Mugwort much in demand by herbalists, in consequence of which it is regularly cultivated in this country, propagation being by division of old perennial plants. The crop in the dry state is worth 20*s.* to 30*s.* per cwt. In the wild state Mugwort is found in hedges and waste places.

Two other members of the same genus are also regularly cultivated in this country for medicinal purposes. These are the Common Wormwood (*Artemisia Absinthium*) and Southernwood (*Artemisia Abrotanum*).

Common Wormwood (*Artemisia Absinthium*).—Its most noticeable characteristics are:—

1. The silkiness of its leaves.
2. The panicles of small heads of dull-yellow flowers at the top of the plant.
3. The aromatic nature of the plant.

This is a plant very common in waste grounds. From it is extracted a volatile oil, consisting chiefly of *absinthol* and *absinthin*; these impart to the oil tonic and febrifuging properties. Wormwood is chiefly used for the manufacture of the French liqueur *absinthe*.

SOUTHERNWOOD (*Artemisia Abrotanum*).—This is a hoary plant, more or less shrubby, with freely divided leaves and yellow flowers. It has a pleasant aroma and taste. Familiar names for it are OLD MAN and BOYS' LOVE. Although commonly cultivated here in our gardens, Southernwood is a native of southern Europe and the temperate parts of Asia. On the Continent a kind of beer is made from the plant. The value of the crop in the dry state is from 20s. to 30s. a cwt.

It should also be mentioned that from SEA WORMWOOD (*Artemisia maritima*), a plant found in salt marshes, a valuable substance called *santonine* is prepared, the supply of which at present comes from Russia. It is a popular remedy for worms, but several cases are on record of children having died from having overdoses administered to them. In addition to giddiness, nausea, and vomiting, santonine turns the urine into a saffron colour, and for many hours everything appears yellow to the vision. In fatal cases, convulsions precede death. Chronic poisoning from santonine is observed in absinthe drinkers. Mr. Shenstone remarks that the value of Sea Wormwood as a source for the extraction of santonine has not yet been investigated; neither have we attempted the cultivation of the Russian variety, from which we obtain our present supply of santonine. At the present moment the price of this drug is prohibitive.

LETTUCE GROUP (*Lactuca*).—The use of the garden Lettuce as an aid to sleep is well known. Another member of this group is LETTUCE OPIUM (*Lactuca virosa*), from which a sedative called *lactucarium* is extracted. This plant is cultivated in this country, and is even found wild in waste, stony places.

THE DANDELION (*Taraxacum officinale*).—Considerable attention is paid nowadays to the collection of this common weed. In normal times English roots were sold, in competition with the German roots, at about 40s a cwt., but two or three months of the War sufficed to raise the price to 110s. a cwt. Naturally the absence of German competition will keep the price high for some time to come.

The root contains a crystalline bitter substance called *taraxacin*, an *acrid resin*, and *mannite*, and is collected in autumn. Whilst not indispensable it is a very valuable drug, as it acts specifically on the liver, increasing and modifying its secretion, and has also a diuretic action.

Cultivation.—It is recommended that 4 lb. of seeds per acre be used, and drilled in rows a foot apart. The roots are dug the second year in autumn.

Collection.—The roots are transported fresh for pressing out the juice, or they may be sliced and dried. If the roots are collected wild, they should be taken from good rather than from poor soil, as those grown from the former are thicker and less forked than those grown from the latter.

The yield in cultivation should be 4 or 5 tons of fresh roots to the acre in the second year. A hundred parts of fresh root yield twenty-two parts of dry material.

BURDOCK (*Arctium Lappa*).—This plant may be mentioned, partly because it had a great reputation in the past, and partly because herbalists still utilize its fruits, seeds, and roots in the exercise of their trade. The root contains *inulin, mucilage sugar*, a bitter glucoside called *lappin*, a little *resin*, and *tannic acid*. It is said to promote the action of the kidneys, and to increase the action of the skin in promoting perspiration.

ELECAMPANE or PLOUGHMAN'S SPIKENARD (*Inula Helenium*).—Among the plants mentioned as worth collecting is Elecampane, the root of which contains 44 per cent of *inulin*, a starch-like compound which in this plant takes the place of starch as a reserve material. In addition it contains a *volatile oil*, an *acrid resin*, and a *bitter principle*. Although the habitat of the plant lies in southern Europe, it grows readily in this country, and by some writers is regarded as a native plant. It can be recognized by the following characteristic points of structure:—

1. The leaves are large, oblong, wrinkled, and egg-shaped.
2. The stem is stouter than the average stem of a plant of this size.
3. The heads of flowers are few in number, very large, and bright-yellow in colour (fig. 85).

Fig. 85.—Elecampane or Ploughman's Spikenard (*Inula Helenium*)

a, Florets.

It flourishes best in moist pastures. As a drug it is cited as a remedy for diseases of the chest and lungs.

MARIGOLD (*Calendula officinalis*).—Although a native of southern Europe, Marigold is especially common in our cottage gardens, being in popular use as a stimulant. It looks like a large yellow or orange-coloured daisy, each floret being about half an inch long. Its odour is somewhat heavy, and its taste bitter. It will grow in any good soil, and should be sown in spring. As Marigold flowers are imported, they must be brought into the search-light which we nowadays bring to bear on all possible useful plants. Mr. Holmes states that the florets require careful drying to prevent them sticking together, and that the commercial article might be much improved by growing a deep-coloured variety, like that known as "Prince of Orange".

Fig. 86.—Common Chamomile (*Anthemis nobilis*)

a, Ray floret. *b*, Disk floret.

The Chamomiles:—

The COMMON CHAMOMILE (*Anthemis nobilis*) is a native of this country, and is cultivated not only here but also in Belgium, France, and elsewhere on the Continent. The flower itself is about ¾ inch in diameter, the ray florets being white, whilst those in the centre are yellow. A further help to identification is provided by the *receptacle*, as is called the platform on which the florets are contained. In contradistinction to the receptacle of the German Chamomile, that of the Common Chamomile is *hollow*, conical, and densely covered with scaly bracts (fig. 86).

The dried expanded flower-heads are collected from cultivated plants, and contain 0·2 per cent of the official volatile oil, and a small amount of a bitter substance. Warm infusions have the general properties of fomentations and poultices, and are much used externally to soothe pain. As it produces a mild emetic effect when taken internally, the plant is used as a cure for biliousness, &c.

GERMAN CHAMOMILE (*Matricaria Chamomilla*).—This plant does not come under the same generic name as the preceding one, and it is only chance which has given these two plants the same common name of Chamomile. The German Chamomile is distinguished by having a *naked receptacle*, that is, the platform bearing the florets is *devoid of scales or bracts*. This readily distinguishes it from the preceding plant. Again, the fruit of the German Chamomile is angular, that of the Common Chamomile round. The former is a native of Central Europe, though it grows wild in this country also, and, if necessary, could easily be cultivated. Its flowers yield a *volatile oil*, a *bitter substance*, and a little *tannic acid*; they are used for the same purpose as the flowers of the Common Chamomile.

There is a considerable demand in this country for Common Chamomile. On the outbreak of war the price rose from 55*s*. a cwt. to 80*s*. per cwt. At the end of August, 1914, it fetched 120*s*. to 140*s*. a cwt. These prices apply to the Belgian crops; the English-grown Chamomile is much dearer even than this, being worth about 3*s*. a pound.

Cultivation of Common Chamomile.—A stiff black loam gives the best results. Each old plant in March is divided into ten or twelve portions: these are planted in rows 2½ feet apart, with a distance of 18 inches between the plants in the row. The flowers are picked in September, rapidly dried, and laid on canvas trays in a heated drying-closet.

YARROW or MILFOIL (*Achillea Millefolium*).—A very common plant on roadsides and pastures and banks. It rises 6–18 inches from the ground, and possesses very finely divided leaves about 2 to 3 inches long (fig. 87).

The flowers are small and white. In identifying this flower, close attention should be paid to the leaves. In former days many healing virtues were ascribed to this herb: chewed in the mouth it cured toothache, applied to the scalp it prevented incipient baldness, and so on.

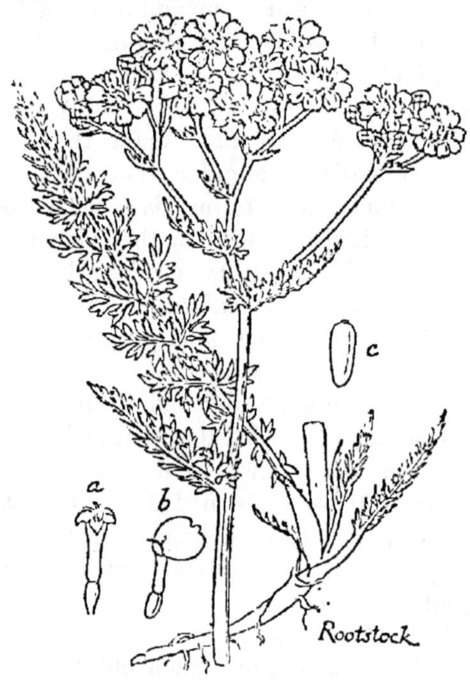

Fig 87.—Yarrow or Milfoil (*Achillea Millefolium*)

a, Disk floret. *b*, Ray floret *c*, Seed.

Whatever its virtues may be, it is still regularly cultivated for medicinal purposes. At present it would pay to extend its cultivation, seeing that we use from 10 to 20 tons of it, the pre-War supply being largely from Germany. Its price has gone up from 20*s*. a cwt. to over 40*s*. a cwt.

Coltsfoot (*Tussilago Farfara*).—This very common weed is often confused by beginners with Dandelion. A glance at the leaves, however, is sufficient to show the marked difference between the two plants. As an

Fig. 88. Coltsfoot (*Tussilago Farfara*)

1. Disk floret. 2. Ray floret. 3. Fruit.

aid to identification it may be noted that a few bracts grow out of the flower-stalk of the Coltsfoot, while that of Dandelion is quite free from such structures.

Formerly the leaves of Coltsfoot were gathered for the manufacture of "tobacco", and as such they are still surreptitiously sold in slum areas as "tobacco" for juveniles (fig. 88). Mixed with Yarrow and Rose leaves, smoked Coltsfoot leaves are said to be good for asthma. They contain *mucilage*, a *bitter glucoside*, and *tannin*. Coltsfoot flowers are imported into this country, a ready sale being found for them among the herbalists.

Fig. 89.—Tansy (*Tanacetum vulgare*)

a, Achene. *b*, Tubular ray floret ☿. *c*, Tubular disk floret ⚥.

The herb grows only too readily in moist clay soils. The leaves are collected in June or July, and the flowers in spring.

Tansy (*Tanacetum vulgare*).—This herb is found throughout Europe, and is very common in our gardens. All the florets are yellow and tubular, forming a head which is rather small and hemispherical. The whole plant grows up to about 2½ feet, and is strongly scented. The leaves are alternate, and very finely divided, each being about 6 inches long.

The extract from Tansy contains *tanacetin*, *tannic acid*, and about 0·2–0·3 per cent of *volatile oil*. In mediæval times this plant was largely employed both for medicinal and for culinary purposes. Medicinally it is used as a stimulant and for promoting the action of the kidneys. Accidents have happened from misuse of the extract on account of its popular reputation for procuring abortion. In one case a woman who took fifteen drops of the oil, and afterwards a teaspoonful, was in convulsions in about a quarter of an hour later. Although this woman recovered, other cases having fatal issues are on record.

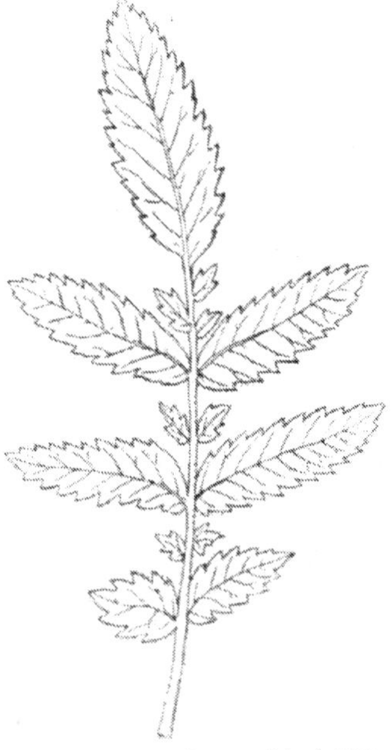

Fig. 90.—Pinnate Leaves of Agrimony (*Agrimonia Eupatorium*)

AGRIMONY (*Agrimonia Eupatorium*).—The flowers are small and yellow, and the leaves are pinnate, the leaflets increasing in size as they near the terminal leaflet (fig. 90). The fragrance is not unlike that of an apricot.

This herb is a very popular one in the stock-in-trade of the herbalists, who sell tons of it during the year. In some rural districts one hears wonderful tales of the potency of this plant as a curative agent, but it is to be feared that its reputation is a legacy bequeathed to us by the "prentice-hands" of the Middle Ages.

We have not exhausted the list of the Composites which are made use of by the herbalists. To those mentioned above we must add RAGWORT (*Senecio Jacobæa*), FEVERFEW (*Chrysanthemum Parthenium*), BUTTERBUR (*Petasites vulgaris*), and a few others. Space does not admit of a detailed consideration of these plants, neither is their importance such as would justify their cultivation and collection.

Rubiaceæ.—Goosegrass Family. This family, in addition to possessing flowers with fused petals and an inferior ovary, has one outstanding feature which is common to all its members, namely the arrangement of its leaves, which are whorled (fig. 91). A plant showing the three characters mentioned above can be placed with certainty among the Rubiaceæ.

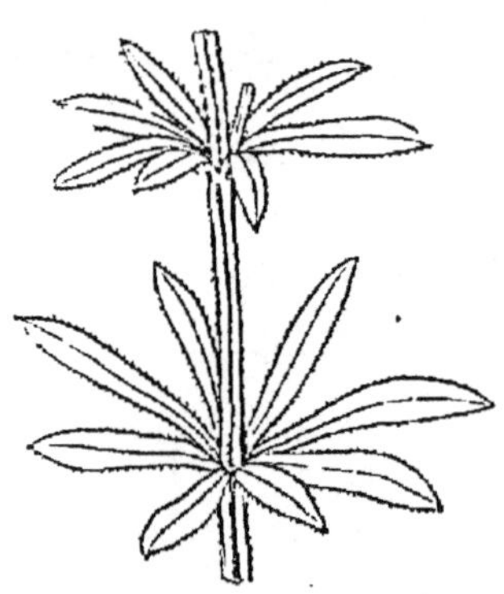

Fig. 91.—Whorled Leaves of Goosegrass Family

GOOSEGRASS, CLEAVERS, CLIVERS (*Galium Aparine*).—This little plant is found scattered in almost every neglected garden and almost every hedge. The prickliness of the stem and leaves is a sufficiently outstanding feature for purposes of recognition, this characteristic being due to the fact that the surfaces of these organs are covered with small hooks of a very tenacious nature. A person brushing through a clump of Goosegrass carries with him many reminders of the plant which are not easy to brush away. The stem is quadrangular, brittle, and jointed; the flowers are few in number, small, and white.

A few generations ago, Goosegrass was an ingredient of all prescriptions for the preparation of cool beverages, at a time when almost every household prepared its own drinks; it was also used for making soothing poultices. Goosegrass is nowadays used for promoting the action of the kidneys and as an anti-scorbutic. It is a plant of first-class importance to the herbalists, who use it very extensively.

Fig. 92.—Goosegrass or Cleavers (*Galium Aparine*)

a, Enlarged edge of leaf, showing hooks.

Woodruff (*Asperula odorata*).—This is another old-fashioned favourite of past generations. It can be easily recognized by the series of bright, shiny whorls of leaves, one above another, as shown in fig. 93. The flowers are minute, ivory-white, and funnel-shaped. The whole plant has an agreeable scent, and in consequence it was used by housewives to impart a pleasant "country" odour to the clean linen in the press, the plant being placed between the folds when the linen was set aside.

Woodruff is especially plentiful in beech woods. It is used by the hundredweight by herbalists, for whom it is gathered in autumn, for it is then that it yields its pleasant odour of new-mown hay.

Caprifoliaceæ.—Honeysuckle Family. There is no single feature in this order which is sufficiently outstanding to arrest attention at once, and so for its identification recourse must be had to a careful examination of the plant with the aid of the table on p. 151. A plant possessing a flower with fused petals, inferior ovary, and not made up of numerous florets of the Daisy pattern, will probably be found to be a member of the Caprifoliaceæ. If the plant is a shrub, the probability is changed into a certainty.

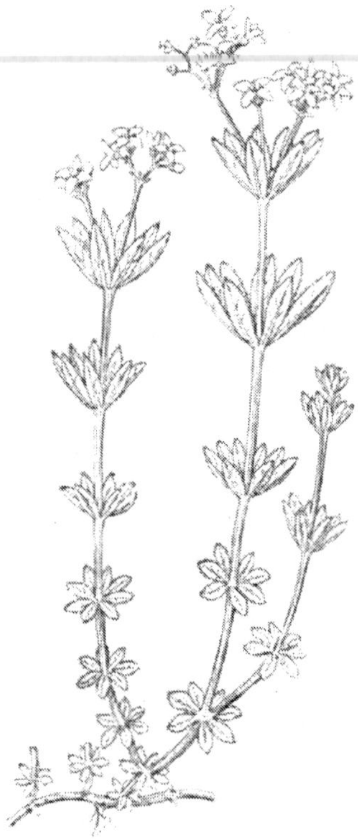

Fig. 93.—Woodruff (*Asperula odorata*)

ELDER (*Sambucus nigra*). See Chap. X.

GUELDER ROSE or SNOWBALL TREE (*Viburnum Opulus*). See Chap. X.

Valerianaceæ.—The Valerian Family. A plant may be included in this family group if—

1. The flowers have fused petals and an inferior ovary.
2. The leaves are not whorled (cf. Woodruff).
3. The plant is a herb, not a shrub.

GREAT WILD VALERIAN (*Valeriana officinalis*).—Of the three genera in this order, the genus Valeriana is distinguished from the others owing to the possession by its members of a corolla which has *only a bulge* at its base instead of a spur (fig. 94). The spur is characteristic of another genus of this order which has no medicinal importance. The Great Wild Valerian stands 3 to 4 feet from the ground, has pink flowers and pinnate leaves (fig. 95). It is very common in England in moist situations, and a part of the drug used in commerce comes from the rhizomes of plants grown in Derbyshire; a large proportion was, however, imported

Fig. 94.—Corolla of Great Wild Valerian

Fig. 95.—Pinnate Leaves of Great Wild Valerian

from Holland, Germany, and France. In January, 1914, the foreign root was selling at 30*s.* a cwt., the English root being worth three or four times that sum. Of late years the cultivation of the English herb has gone down owing to foreign competition, so that at the present time there is a great scarcity, and for some time to come abnormal prices are likely to be paid. We use about 10 tons annually, and of this about a tenth is grown in this country. When in addition it is stated that the Valerian is an indispensable plant, it will readily be seen that cogent reasons exist for its renewed cultivation in this country. The Jap Valerian has lately come into the market at about 200*s.* a cwt.

Cultivation.—Young flowering wild plants which develop at the end of slender runners that are given off by the perennial runners, are usually chosen for transplanting. These are planted on land treated with farmyard manure. It is advantageous to give plenty of liquid manure and artificial manure from time to time. The plants are also given plenty of water. As only the rhizomes are collected, the flowering tops are cut off as much as possible in order to encourage the growth of the rhizome. In September or October the tops are cut off with a scythe, and the rhizomes allowed to be dug up. These are sliced longitudinally to facilitate washing, washed thoroughly, and dried on a shed floor about 6 feet from the ground. The wet material is strewn on perforated boards, below which a large coke stove is kept going until the drying is complete. About 24 parts of the dry product are obtained from 100 parts of fresh rhizome.

Properties.—From the rhizome about ½ to 1 per cent of a *volatile oil*, containing *pinene*, *camphene*, *borneol*, and various *esters*, is obtained. The pungent taste and peculiarly disagreeable odour of the oil are sometimes valuable aids to the military doctor when he has to prescribe for the complaints of "old soldiers". Apart from this, Valerian is a powerful carminative, a *circulatory stimulant*, and an *antispasmodic*. It is used in cases of hysterical flatulence, fainting, palpitations, &c. Other uses are indicated by the name "All-heal" which is sometimes given to it, on account of its frequent use by the poor to cure flesh wounds.

TABLE IV

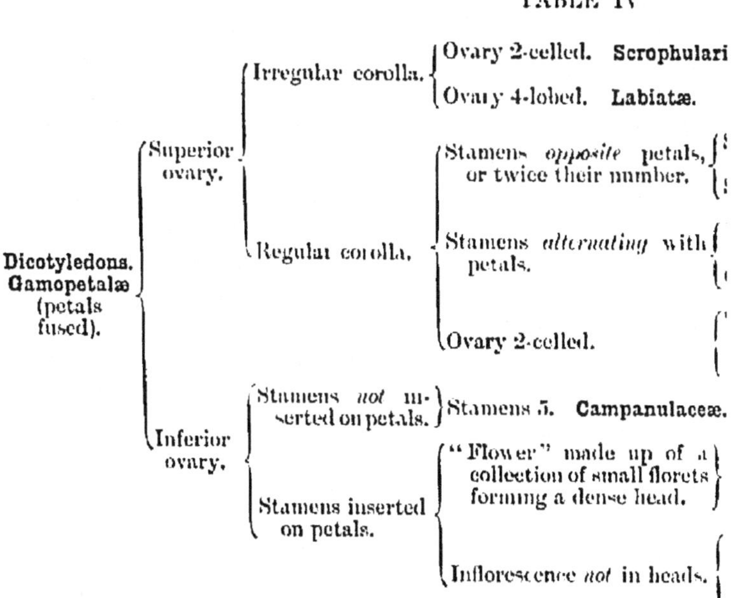
Dicotyledons.
Gamopetalæ
(petals
fused).
Superior
ovary.
Irregular corolla.
Ovary 2-celled. Scrophulari
Ovary 4-lobed. Labiatæ.
Regular corolla.
Stamens opposite petals, or twice their number.
Stamens alternating with petals.
Ovary 2-celled.
Inferior
ovary.
Stamens not inserted on petals.
Stamens 5. Campanulaceæ.
Stamens inserted on petals.
"Flower" made up of a collection of small florets forming a dense head.
Inflorescence not in heads.

CHAPTER X

TREES AND SHRUBS

In this chapter we have grouped together the trees and large shrubs of medicinal value or of a poisonous nature. It must be emphasized that the plants therein contained have no necessary relationship, and have been grouped together as a matter of convenience; the difficulty in identifying a plant is lessened considerably if it is known to be either a tree or a shrub. All the main groups are represented, with the exception of the Monocotyledons. In addition to the groups discussed above, a few of the trees and shrubs of medicinal importance or of a poisonous nature belong to the Gymnosperms, the lowest group of Flowering Plants, and one which includes the Pines, Larches, Cedars, &c. All the Gymnosperms are trees and shrubs, and for our purpose we can pick out any particular one more easily by directing our attention to points of structure peculiar to it, rather than by drawing up tables such as have served our purpose usefully in regard to the Monocotyledons and Dicotyledons.

THE OAK (*Quercus Robur*).—The bark of young trees (up to about twenty years old) is used medicinally as an astringent, on account of the large amount of *tannin* which it contains. Longitudinal incisions are made in spring through the bark so that it can be removed in strips. These, after being dried, are ready for the market. On the Continent, in some districts, cattle which have been kept indoors throughout the winter are liberated in the spring, at the time as it happens when the young leaves of the Oak have not yet developed the tannin which later appears in them. The cattle browse greedily on the young leaves, a proceeding which later results in a disease known as *maladie des bois*.[1] The animals lie down for long intervals; fever and other troubles follow, and in some cases death ensues. The cause appears to be the particular substances present in the young leaves of the Oak which later develop into *tannin*.

THE BEECH (*Fagus sylvatica*).—The Beech is recognized by—

1. The shape of the leaves (fig. 96, *a*).
2. The cigar-shaped brown buds (fig. 96, *b*).
3. The smooth bark.

The fruit is known as *beechmast*, and consists of two triangular, hard brown nutlets, sitting upright on a four-

Fig. 96.—*a*, Beech Leaf. *b*, Buds of Beech. *c*, Beech Nut.

lobed platform (fig. 96, *c*). The husk of the nut was formerly made into a cake for feeding cattle, because it contains a quantity of nutritious oil. But it contains also a deleterious substance which is poisonous, so that the husks have long since been given up as a food. The leaves of the Beech are not injurious to browsing animals.

THE YEW (*Taxus baccata*).—This funereal-looking plant belongs to the Gymnosperms and calls for careful consideration, as it is reckoned to be the most dangerous

[1] It may be mentioned here that this malady is also caused when the young leaves of the Hornbeam, Furze, Broom, or Hazel are eaten by animals.

tree for cattle that we possess in Great Britain. It is commonly found in burial-places, and the reason for this is alleged to be, that as the preservation of the Yew in the Middle Ages was a matter of importance, because its branches were used for the making of bows, the burial-

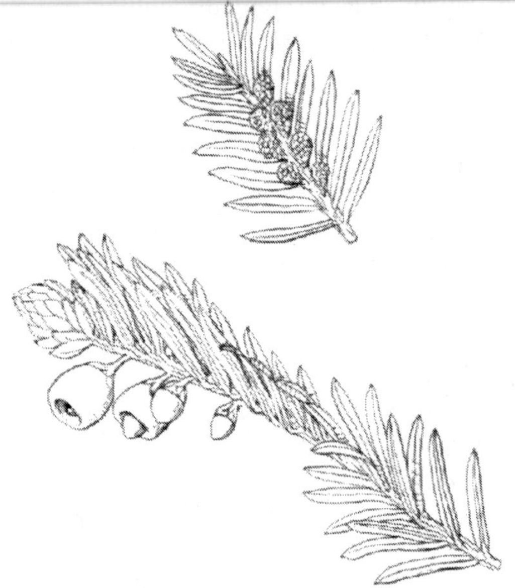

Fig. 97.—Leaves and Berries of Yew

ground was chosen on account of its sanctity, which would probably ensure a freedom from damage to all the plants growing within the enclosure.

The Yew is not difficult to recognize.

1. The leaves are so arranged that they all approximately lie in one plane. Each is about $\frac{3}{4}$ to 1 inch long, and about $\frac{1}{8}$ of this in width (fig. 97).
2. Scarlet "berries"[1].

[1] The word *berry* is used here in a popular sense. Botanically the term has a precise definition, to which the "berry" of the Yew does not conform.

As drying does not weaken the poisonous properties of the leaves, and as there is no warning signal in the form of an unpleasant taste or smell, the leaves and berries constitute a real danger to cattle and to children. In winter especially, cattle will readily browse on the leaves. Not only the leaves and berries, but also the wood and bark are poisonous, although the leaves, and especially the older ones, are the most dangerous. One case is on record in which three horses, taken to be sold at a country fair, had been tethered to the churchyard railings, and had whilst there eaten Yew boughs: all three died from the effects There are records which show that not only horses, but asses, cows, and rabbits have been poisoned by this plant. The scarlet covering to the seed is not harmful *when ripe*, but the seed itself is deadly poisonous. It is said that on one occasion on which thirty-two persons had by accident partaken of Yew seeds and leaves, twenty died of the poison. Henslow states that several cases are on record of inmates of lunatic asylums having died after chewing Yew leaves. The active principles are a bitter alkaloid called *taxine*, which evolves an aromatic odour, and a crystalline alkaloid called *milossine*.

This is the first example of the Gymnosperms with which we have become acquainted. Most of the members of this group possess long needle-like leaves, a characteristic which imparts to most of them a funereal appearance; this is possibly the reason for their frequent appearance in burial grounds. Other examples besides the Yew are the Scotch Pine, the Fir, which is selected for our "Christmas-tree", the Cypress, and the Larch.

THE COMMON JUNIPER (*Juniperus communis*).—This is also one of the Gymnosperms, and possesses the characteristic needle-like leaves. It can be distinguished from the other Gymnosperms by—

1. The leaves, which are arranged either in whorls of three or in an "opposite" arrangement (fig. 98).
2. The *berries*, which have a dark purple colour and are covered by a whitish bloom. They measure about $\frac{1}{3}$ inch in diameter. At the apex is a scar which radiates in three directions, whilst at the base are some six minute scaly structures in two whorls. Inside of the berry will be found three triangular seeds.

The slight turpentine odour associated with gin and Hollands (a spirit prepared from corn) is due to the flavouring of these spirits with the juice of Juniper berries. This juice contains a powerful stimulant, acting especially on the kidneys. This diuretic action of the extract is made use of in combating dropsy. The ripe berry contains about 1 per cent of *volatile oil* and a considerable quantity of *sugar*.

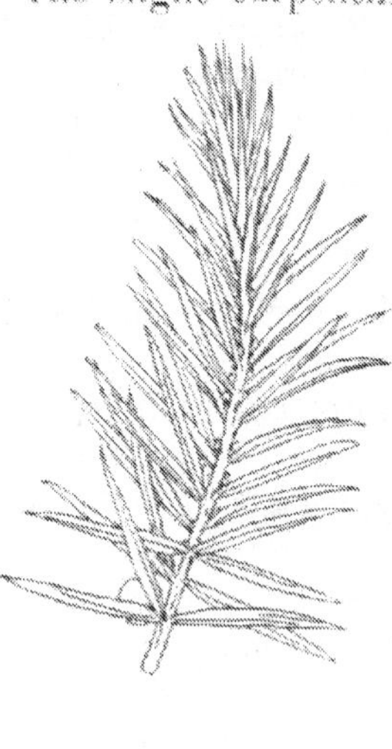

Fig. 98.—Leaves of Juniper

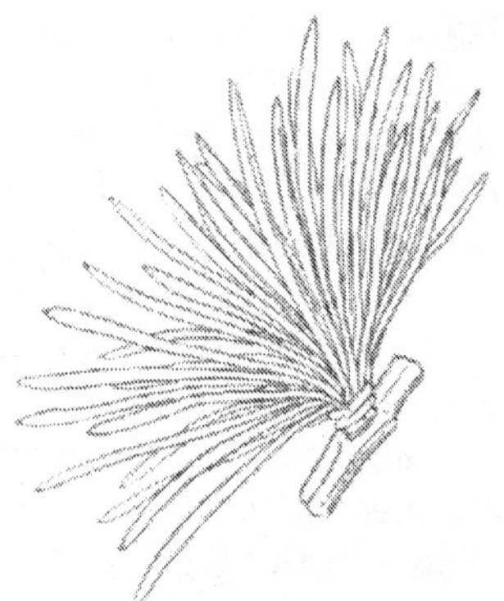

Fig. 99.—Leaves of Larch

THE LARCH (*Abies Larix*).—The Larch is a familiar

Gymnosperm in our country, and is easily identified by the fact of the leaves not being scattered all over the stem, but arranged in little communities, each composed of twenty or more needle-like leaves (fig. 99). The bark contains *tannin* and a crystalline substance called *laricin* which has a bitter astringent taste. Its use as a stimulant, expectorant, and astringent is almost obsolete.

LABURNUM (*Cytisus Laburnum* — Natural Order **Leguminosæ**).—This is not of British origin, but it has

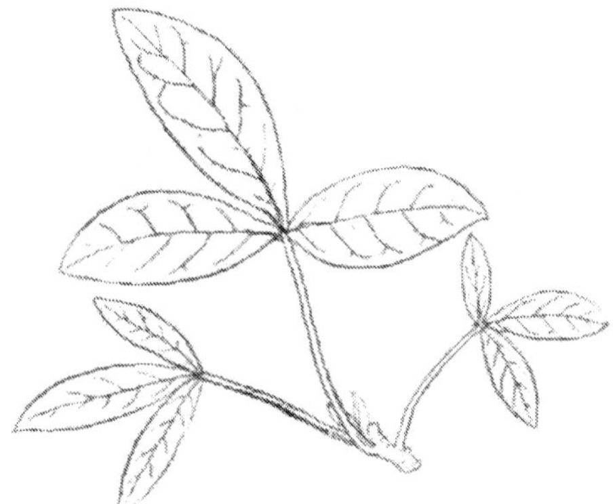

Fig. 100.—Laburnum Leaves

now become one of the most familiar of our garden growths. It may also be regarded as one of the most poisonous among them. The yellow leguminous flower seen on a shrub or small tree is sufficient to identify the plant as Laburnum; to make sure, the leaves should be compared with fig. 100.

Poisonous Properties.—All parts are harmful, and particularly the seeds. The bright colour of the flowers attracts small children, the sweetness of the roots reminds boys of the taste of liquorice, whilst the seeds have a certain resemblance to pea-seeds; consequently we cannot be surprised at the large number of cases of Laburnum poisoning which are continually occurring. In most cases in which a medical man is called to attend, it is the seeds that have been eaten. The signs of Laburnum poisoning are vomiting, pains in the stomach, and general prostration. The active principle is an alkaloid called *cytisine*, of which there is about 3 per cent in the seeds. This substance has a bitter and acrid taste, and causes dilatation of the eye-pupil.

The Almond Group (Amygdalæ).—The Almond tree itself is not a native of this country, although it flowers and even forms fruit in the South of England; better representatives are the **Laurel, Peach,** and **Sloe.** This group calls for careful study, as an insidious poison is to be found in most of its members. Fortunately the fruits of all, with the exception of the Laurel, are not only non-poisonous, but furnish nutritious foods. The poison resides chiefly in the leaves; or rather, a substance called *amygdalin* is found in the leaves which is not poisonous itself, but under certain circumstances becomes changed into *prussic acid.* The chemical change which takes place is as follows:—

Amygdalin + Water = Benzaldehyde
+ Glucose + *Prussic Acid.*

This chemical change can take place only if a ferment called *emulsin* is present. This ferment does not itself take part in the reaction, but supplies, as it were, the energy, without which the reaction cannot take place. Any plant, or part of a plant, therefore, which forms amygdalin must be regarded with suspicion, for in the metabolism of the plant, in the natural course of events, at some period, emulsin must also be produced; for amygdalin, which is a reserve food-material, is of no use to the plant until it has been changed into glucose, no more than starch is of any use to our own bodies until it has been changed to some form of sugar; and emulsin is the specific ferment which the plant develops, in order to accomplish this change in the amygdalin. So far as the seeds are concerned the danger is not great, unless they are eaten after they have commenced to germinate, or after they have been bruised. But on several occasions cattle have suffered, and it has happened in this way. In the manufacture of oil of almonds, the refuse, still containing much oil, is pressed into cakes and served as food to cattle. In this food the change mentioned above sometimes takes place, and the cattle fed on it are poisoned. A verdict of manslaughter was returned against a clergyman who had prescribed and administered oil of bitter almonds to one of his parishioners. This oil contains from 8 to 15 per cent of prussic acid. *Essence of Almonds* is also very poisonous. For the reason given above, concoctions which give an almond flavour to the products of the confectioner's art are not without danger. The leaves of the Peach, the Plum, and the Cherry are to be regarded as poisonous; in fact, the leaves of every member of this sub-division must be regarded with suspicion, because the formation of amygdalin seems to occur throughout the family. One member demands special treatment on account of its importance both as a poison and as a medicine.

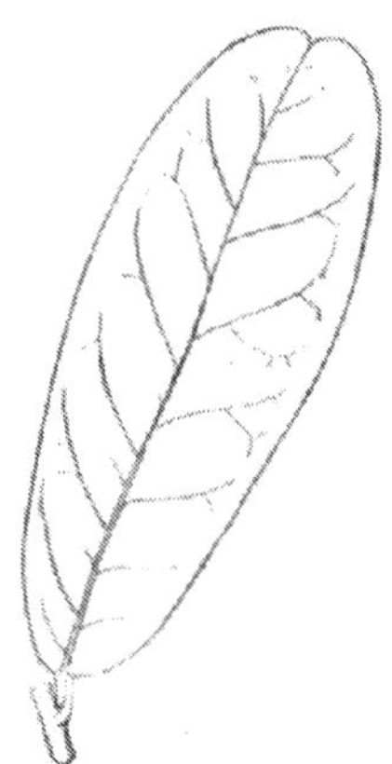

Fig. 101.—Laurel Leaf

COMMON LAUREL or CHERRY LAUREL (*Prunus Laurocerasus*).—The shrub is very common, and is readily recognized by its leaves. These are 5 to 7 inches long, somewhat oblong in form, and possessing a very short stalk. They are thick, coriaceous, dark-green, smooth, having a shining upper surface: on the under side the colour is of a paler hue (fig. 101). Near the base are one or two glandular depressions. When bruised the leaves give out an odour resembling that of bitter almonds. Laurel leaves are used with great success for flavouring custards; but it must be noted, first, that the very vapour arising from them is destructive to insect life, and secondly, *laurel-water* is a very poisonous liquid. In the case of this plant the potentially dangerous substance is not amygdalin, but a closely allied glucoside called *lauro-cerasin*, which also changes into prussic acid by the intervention of the appropriate ferment. The preparation called *Aqua Lauro-cerasi* is made from the fresh leaves of the Laurel, and contains 1 to 10 per cent prussic acid. The danger arises from the fact that there can be no absolute certainty of the amount of change into prussic acid that may have taken place in the lauro-cerasin of any part of the Laurel that is being used. There is said to be more prussic acid in leaves gathered in cold and wet weather than in those picked when the weather is hot and dry. Again, the Continental species of Laurel yields more prussic acid than the British plant.

Whilst laurel-water is decidedly poisonous, and whilst there are records against the leaves from the Continent as having caused the death of sheep and oxen, we have to state that Henslow mentions the fact that his cows ruined a long laurel hedge without any ill effects to themselves. This only serves to emphasize the variable nature in the occurrence of the poison in this plant.

Medicinal uses.—The principal use for cherry-laurel water is for flavouring; it is also used as a sedative, prussic acid in *very small* quantities producing this effect on the human system.

Before leaving the Almond group it is necessary to state that the following should be regarded as being potentially or actively dangerous: Plum kernels; flowers and fruit of Wild Service Tree (*Pyrus Torminalis*); kernels of Cherry; kernels of Apple; flowers and kernels of Sloe (*Prunus spinosa*); kernels of Gean Cherry (*Prunus Avium*); kernels of Damson, Peach, and Apricot.

Fig. 102 —Spurge Laurel (*Daphne Laureola*)

THE BAY LAUREL (*Laurus nobilis*) —This plant may suitably be dealt with here, on account of its similarity, superficially, to the above, although the Bay Laurel is not a member of the Almond group, or even of the Rosaceæ. It is distinguished by having shining, *purple-ribbed* green leaves, lance-shaped or more pointed, and with a wavy margin. When bruised they emit an *aromatic odour*, and this is the character which is most useful in distinguishing the Bay from the Cherry Laurel.

Medicinal Properties.—The leaves are aromatic and stimulant, and the plant is quoted in Mr. Holmes's list of plants used by herbalists in large quantities. The leaves are collected from May to September.

THE SPURGE LAUREL (*Daphne Laureola*)—There is

no relationship between this plant and either of the two foregoing plants, for the Spurge Laurel is a member of an order called *Thymeleaceæ*, which is included in the Gamopetalæ. It is mentioned here, however, because some confusion seems to exist as to the plants included under the term "Laurel". The flowers and leaf of the Spurge Laurel are shown in fig. 102. The bark is acrid, laxative, and poisonous, and has been used for the cure of cutaneous, rheumatic, and venereal diseases. Whilst birds seem to feed with impunity on the fruits, the latter are poisonous to other animals, including man.

ELDER (*Sambucus nigra*—Natural Order **Caprifoliaceæ.**)—This is a very useful shrub, and is as common as it is useful. It is easily recognized as a shrub by its large pinnate leaves, which have a somewhat unpleasant odour. The white flowers, superficially regarded, appear to be arranged as an *umbel*; but this is found, on closer examination, not to be the case, as the stalks of the little flowers do not rise from the same level, although all attain approximately the same height. In autumn these flowers form black berries of lustrous hue. The Elder is sometimes confused with the Rowan, but in winter the birch-like trunk, and in autumn the red berries, of the latter are sufficiently outstanding features to prevent mistakes.

The young leaf-buds are very purgative, and are therefore to be regarded as somewhat poisonous organs, and the same properties belong to the bark. The juice of the root proved fatal to a woman who had partaken of it as a supposed remedy for a bilious attack. The leaves also are poisonous; in one instance, at least, a child is known to have been poisoned by eating the leaves. Lastly, the berries are very purgative, although their bitter taste is a deterrent to all except the most abnormal of tastes. Medicinally the flowers are gathered for the preparation of elder-flower water, a fluid that is used in the mixing of medicines, and which is in addition a gentle stimulant. Elderberry wine is a beverage of a not very exciting nature, which politeness sometimes compels us to drink.

Fig. 163.—Common Elder: Foliage, Inflorescence, and Fruit

The fragrance of the flowers is due to the presence of a nearly solid, volatile oil and to some volatile acids. We use about 5 tons of the plant, practically all supplied from Germany, although recently France and England have been tapped. The price has increased from 70*s.* to 120*s.* a cwt. since the beginning of the War. The flowers should be collected when *nearly* mature, as the corollas only are used, and these fall off very easily when the flowers are mature. The Board of Agriculture recommends a quick collection and rapid transit of the flowers if they are to be used for making elder-flower water. They can be preserved for future distillation by mixing them with 10 per cent of common salt.

Guelder Rose or Snowball Tree (*Viburnum Opulus*).—A medicinal use is made of the bark of this old-fashioned shrub, easily recognized by its spherical clusters of white flowers, not unlike small snowballs in appearance. The extract from the bark is used as a tonic and diuretic.

APPENDIX

The Board of Agriculture and Fisheries has recently issued a leaflet (No. 288) in which much information is given concerning the medicinal herbs which from considerations either of patriotism or profit should be grown in this country. Most attention is given to the following plants:—

Aconite (*Aconitum Napellus*).
Belladonna (*Atropa Belladonna*).
Chamomile (*Anthemis nobilis*).
Dandelion (*Taraxacum officinale*).
Dill (*Peucedanum graveolens*).
"Egyptian Henbane" (*Datura Metel*)
Fennel (*Fœniculum capillaceum*).
Foxglove (*Digitalis purpurea*).
Golden Seal (*Hydrastis canadensis*).
Henbane (*Hyoscyamus niger*).
Opium Poppy (*Papaver somniferum*).
Thorn Apple (*Datura Stramonium*).
Valerian (*Valeriana officinalis*).

Whilst the above are the most important, it is also pointed out that the following are regularly cultivated for the market in this country:—

Balm (*Melissa officinalis*).
Comfrey (*Symphytum officinale*).
Feverfew (*Chrysanthemum Parthenium*).
Germander (*Teucrium Scorodonia*).

Greater Celandine (*Chelidonium majus*).
Marsh Mallow (*Althæa officinalis*).
Mugwort (*Artemisia vulgaris*).
Pennyroyal (*Mentha Pulegium*).
Rue (*Ruta graveolens*).
Southernwood (*Artemisia Abrotanum*).
Tansy (*Tanacetum vulgare*).
Wormwood (*Artemisia Absinthium*).
Yarrow (*Achillea Millefolium*).

The value of the crops in the dry state from these plants reaches from 20*s*. to 30*s*. a cwt. In a third list attention is drawn to plants which, though not regularly cultivated, are quite common as wild or garden plants, and are in great demand by herbalists and pharmacists:—

Barberry (*Berberis vulgaris*).
Bittersweet (*Solanum Dulcamara*).
Broom (*Cytisus Scoparius*).
Buck-bean or Bog-bean (*Menyanthes trifoliata*).
Burdock (*Arctium Lappa*).
Centaury (*Erythræa Centaurium*).
Coltsfoot (*Tussilago Farfara*).
Elder (*Sambucus nigra*).
Figwort (*Scrophularia nodosa*).
Hemlock (*Conium maculatum*).
Horehound (*Marrubium vulgare*).
Male Fern (*Nephrodium* (*Aspidium*) *Filix-Mas*).
Meadow Saffron (*Colchicum autumnale*).
Meadow-sweet (*Spiræa Ulmaria*).
Mullein (*Verbascum Thapsus*).
Red Poppy (*Papaver Rhœas*).
Rose petals.
Sweet Flag (*Acorus Calamus*).
Yarrow (*Achillea Millefolium*).

A valuable article on the same lines has appeared in

the *Pharmaceutical Journal* from the pen of Mr E. M. Holmes, in which the whole situation with regard to the cultivation of medicinal plants is brought under review. It is evident that a prospective grower of medicinal plants will have to take many things into consideration before launching his capital into the enterprise. Not only must the price of land be very cheap (about 10s. an acre), but cheap labour must be secured, and care taken that the soil is suitable for the herb that it is proposed to grow. Further, he must acquaint himself with the fungi and other parasites that are likely to do damage to his crops.

In List 1 in this article are included those plants which are abundant, and "are wanted by the hundredweight, and in some cases by the ton":—

Agrimony (*Agrimonia Eupatoria*).
Avens (*Geum urbanum*).
Broom (*Cytisus Scoparius*).
Buckbean (*Menyanthes trifoliata*).
Burdock (*Arctium Lappa*).
Centaury (*Erythræa Centaurium*),
Clivers (*Galium Aparine*).
Comfrey (*Symphytum officinale*).
Dandelion (*Taraxacum officinale*).
Equisetum (*Equisetum arvense*).
Eyebright (*Euphrasia officinalis*).
Figwort (*Scrophularia nodosa*).
Fumitory (*Fumaria officinalis*).
Greater Burnet (*Sanguisorba officinalis*).
Greater Celandine (*Chelidonium majus*).
Ground Ivy (*Glechoma hederacea*).
Hemlock (*Conium maculatum*).
Meadow-sweet (*Spiræa Ulmaria*).
Mountain Flax (*Linum catharticum*).
Mugwort (*Artemisia vulgaris*).
Mullein (*Verbascum Thapsus*).

Ragwort (*Senecio Jacobæa*).
Raspberry (*Rubus Idæus*).
Sanicle (*Sanicula Europæa*).
Vervain (*Verbena officinalis*).
Wild Carrot (*Daucus Carota*).
Wood Betony (*Stachys Betonica*).
Wood Sage (*Teucrium Scorodonia*).
Yarrow (*Achillea Millefolium*).

In List 2 the names are given of those plants that are required by the hundredweight, but are not abundant, being found only locally:—

Belladonna (*Atropa Belladonna*).
Chamomile (*Anthemis nobilis*).
Feverfew (*Chrysanthemum Parthenium*).
Foxglove (*Digitalis purpurea*).
Germander (*Teucrium Chamædrys*).
Marsh Mallow (*Althæa officinalis*).
Melilot (*Melilotus officinalis*).
Motherwort (*Leonurus cardiaca*).
Pennyroyal (*Mentha Pulegium*).
Peppermint (*Mentha piperita*).
Sundew (*Drosera rotundifolia*).
Tansy (*Tanacetum vulgare*).
Woodruff (*Asperula odorata*).
Wormwood (*Artemisia Absinthium*).

In a third table is given a list of plants, known as sweet herbs, that are not natives of this country, but grow readily in our gardens, and are in great demand by herbalists. List 3:—

Angelica (*Angelica Archangelica*).
Balm (*Melissa officinalis*).
Basil (*Ocimum Basilicum*).
Bay Tree (*Laurus nobilis*).
Hyssop (*Hyssopus officinalis*).

Lemon Thyme (*Thymus citriodorus*).
Mint (*Mentha viridis*).
Parsley (*Carum Petroselinum*).
Red and White Sage (*Salvia officinalis*).
Rue (*Ruta graveolens*).
Southernwood (*Artemisia Abrotanum*).
Sweet Marjoram (*Origanum Majorana*).
Tarragon (*Artemisia Dracunculus*).
Thyme (*Thymus vulgaris*).

In a fourth list, *flowers* of medicinal interest are tabulated:—

Broom (*Cytisus Scoparius*).
Chamomile (*Anthemis nobilis*).
Coltsfoot (*Tussilago Farfara*).
Cornflower (*Centaurea Cyanus*).
Cowslip (*Primula veris*).
Elder (*Sambucus nigra*).
Hollyhock (*Althaea rosea*).
Lavender (*Lavandula vera*).
Lily of the Valley (*Convallaria majalis*).
Lime Tree (*Tilia europaea*).
Mallow (*Malva sylvestris*).
Marigold (*Calendula officinalis*).
Marsh Mallow (*Althaea officinalis*).
Mullein (*Verbascum Thapsus*).
Red Clover (*Trifolium pratense*).
Rose (*Rosa gallica*).
Violet (*Viola odorata*).

Among the *fruits* and *seeds*, the collection of which would repay the trouble of cultivation, we find the following:—

Angelica (*Archangelica officinalis*).
Black Mustard (*Brassica nigra*).
Broom (*Cytisus Scoparius*).

Burdock (*Arctium Lappa*).
Caraway (*Carum Carvi*).
Celery (*Apium graveolens*).
Colchicum (*Colchicum autumnale*).
Coriander (*Coriandrum sativum*).
Dandelion (*Taraxacum officinale*).
Dill (*Peucedanum graveolens*).
Fennel (*Fœniculum dulce*).
Flea Seed (*Plantago Psyllium*).
Fœnugreek (*Trigonella Fœnum-græcum*).
Hemlock (*Conium maculatum*).
Linseed (*Linum usitatissimum*).
Mawseed (*Papaver somniferum*).
Quince (*Pyrus Cydonia*).
Stramonium (*Datura Stramonium*).
White Mustard (*Brassica alba*).

Finally, among the *roots* that are worth collecting and drying, the following are the most important. It is to be noted that the term "root" is used here in its popular sense, and includes underground stems as well as the structures that botanically are included under this term:—

Bistort (*Polygonum Bistorta*).
Black Bryony (*Tamus communis*).
Burnet (*Pimpinella Saxifraga*).
Butterbur (*Petasites vulgaris*).
Calamus (*Acorus Calamus*).
Colchicum (*Colchicum autumnale*).
Couch Grass (*Agropyrum repens*).
Curled Dock (*Rumex crispus*).
Elecampane (*Inula Helenium*).
Gladwin (*Iris fœtidissima*).
Horseradish (*Cochlearia Armoracia*).
Lovage (*Levisticum officinale*).
Male Fern (*Nephrodium (Aspidium) Filix-Mas*).
Polypody (*Polypodium vulgare*).

(Red) Dock (*Rumex aquaticus*).
Tormentil (*Potentilla Tormentilla*).

The author is indebted to Mr. Holmes for kind permission to quote the foregoing lists. Reprints of his paper may be obtained from Mr. Holmes (Ruthven, Sevenoaks, Kent) Bulletin 78 of the West of Scotland Agricultural College, written by Mr. Hosking, may be perused with profit by all who are interested in medicinal plants.

In a lecture delivered before the Royal Society of Arts on 2nd May, 1917, Mr. J. C. Shenstone has given us some useful hints with regard to the policy which we should pursue in the near future in order to make herb growing profitable in this country and safe from the attacks of foreign competitors. Just as the cultivated strawberry has been derived from the wild strawberry by careful cultivation, so it is probable that an increase in the percentage of the active principles of our drug plants could be obtained by their careful cultivation under optimum conditions. It is not to be expected that this will be possible without State aid, for, financially, the experimental cultivation of drug herbs is certain to be conducted at a loss, and it is fitting that the State should pay for results that would benefit all growers. Mr. Shenstone instances how the alkaloidal value of *cinchona bark* was greatly raised by cultivation. A still more remarkable instance of the effect of cultivation is supplied by the fact that English henbane is very much richer in alkaloids than the same plant grown in Germany. This plant appears to be very erratic in its growth, sometimes refusing to grow altogether, and the few growers who have discovered the secret of the conditions of its growth prefer not to disclose them. Again, it has been found that foxglove growing on a hot sandy bank, protected by a wood, gives digitalis of the highest physiological value. There can be little doubt of the soundness of these views. Here we have three cases—cinchona, henbane, and foxglove—in which we have already had results by observation and by experimental cultivation, and there can be little doubt that if the whole problem of our drugs were taken up by the Government, results of no mean value would swiftly accrue.

A further line of policy would be the experimental cultivation of plants which have never hitherto been exploited for medicinal purposes, although it is known that they grow readily in this country. Thus, liquorice (*Glycyrrhiza glabra*) is grown in Yorkshire, though our supply comes from Spain and Italy. Saffron (stigmata and styles of *Crocus sativus*) was formerly grown at Saffron Walden in Essex, but we import it now from Spain. Alkanet root, which was grown in England, comes now chiefly from Hungary. Other examples of medicinal plants of this category are the rhizome of Orris (*Iris florentina, Iris pallida, Iris germanica*), Sweet Flag (*Acorus Calamus*), Cummin fruit (*Cuminum Cyminum*), Wintergreen (*Gaultheria procumbens*), *Lobelia inflata, Podophyllum peltatum, Hydrastis canadensis, Artemisia maritima*, which yields santonine.

If we push this development to its logical conclusion it will be necessary to take under consideration the whole gamut of the drugs that appear on the market, and secure their cultivation in one or other of our colonies.

INDEX

A

B

C

D

E

F

G

H

CPSIA information can be obtained
at www.ICGtesting.com
Printed in the USA
LVHW081736220719
624865LV00009B/66/P

9 781376 347531